THE ROYAL SCOTS

THE ROYAL SCOTS

TREVOR ROYLE

A Concise History

MAINSTREAM
PUBLISHING

EDINBURGH AND LONDON

First published in Great Britain in 2006 by
MAINSTREAM PUBLISHING COMPANY (EDINBURGH) LTD
7 Albany Street
Edinburgh EH1 3UG

ISBN 1 84596 088 2

A catalogue record for this book is available from the British Library

Typeset in Ernhardt and Univers

Printed in Great Britain by
William Clowes Ltd, Beccles, Suffolk

CONTENTS

PREFACE

In 2006 The Royal Regiment of Scotland came into being. Through an imaginative piece of military planning its formation day was 28 March, the same date as the foundation of its oldest antecedent regiment, The Royal Scots. In the same year The Royal Scots amalgamated with The King's Own Scottish Borderers to form the 1st battalion of the new regiment. Inevitably the changes created a great deal of sadness in the army community and more widely throughout Scotland, with regret being expressed for the loss of some cherished names and the conversion of regiments into a new formation. However, the history of the British Army shows that the story of its regiments has been one of constant development, with cutbacks, amalgamations and changes of name being part of a process of evolution stretching back over several centuries. In every case the development has not led to a diminution of the army's capabilities but has produced new regiments which are the equal of their predecessors.

Together with the other books in the series, this concise history has been written to mark this latest transformation in Scottish and British military history. It is not a new regimental history of The Royal Scots but I hope it will be a useful addition to the regiment's historiography. I owe a tremendous debt to previous regimental historians, whose books are listed in the bibliography, especially to Lieutenant-Colonel Robert H. Paterson whose

Pontius Pilate's Bodyguard: A History of the First or the Royal Regiment of Foot, The Royal Scots (The Royal Regiment) is a model of its kind and a great source of inspiration. For help with sources and illustrations, I would like to thank the Regimental Secretary Colonel R.P. Mason. The regiment also kindly agreed to the use of copyright material in its possession. Grateful thanks are also due to Major-General Mark Strudwick, who gave his blessing to the project during his period of office as Colonel of the Regiment.

Trevor Royle

ONE

PONTIUS PILATE'S BODYGUARD

Whatever hand history might choose to deal to The Royal Scots in the future, it cannot change one unassailable fact: they are the oldest regiment in the British Army with a history of service to 17 British monarchs – from King Charles I to Queen Elizabeth II – and a list of battle honours which stretches back to the seventeenth century. One other irrefutable fact gives colour to the regiment's story: because it has its origins in European service it has also served two French kings, Louis XIII and Louis XIV. No other British regiment can lay claim to such a legacy, although two English regiments, 5th Foot (later Royal Northumberland Fusiliers) and 6th Foot (later Royal Warwickshire Fusiliers) began their careers in Dutch service. Until The Royal Scots amalgamated with The King's Own Scottish Borderers in 2006 to form the 1st battalion of The Royal Regiment of Scotland it was numbered 1st in the army's order of precedence and stood in the honoured position, 'Right of the Line'. At the time of its transformation, it was also one of only four British line infantry regiments which could lay claim to never having been amalgamated during the army's many periods

9

of change between the seventeenth and twenty-first centuries. The others were The Green Howards (19th), The Cheshire Regiment (22nd) and The King's Own Scottish Borderers (25th).

However, it is the longevity of The Royal Scots which gives it its special place in military history. It can trace its origins back to 1633, when Sir John Hepburn of Athelstaneford, an experienced soldier in French service, received a warrant from the Privy Council of Scotland, issued under the authority of King Charles I, to raise 1,200 recruits in Scotland. The King signed the documents on 28 March, the date which marks the regiment's foundation; presciently, it was also the year when the new King of Britain agreed to come north from London to be crowned in his Scottish capital. It was a decision which had long been anticipated in Scotland, for Charles had spent most of his childhood in London, having been taken there as a child when his father assumed the English throne to become King James I of Britain. After succeeding his father in 1625, Charles made it clear that he had little time for his northern subjects and made few attempts to understand them or to give substance to their political and religious aspirations. There was also a question of style. Despite his heritage – Charles could write and speak in his native Scottish tongue with the best of them – the Scots seemed to be an alien people, their nobles rough-mannered and uncouth, so different from the formality of the court in London with its ordered refinement and cultural pretensions. In short, Charles considered the Scots to be boorish, almost comically so, and he shied away from their over-familiarity, finding them backward, sullen and lacking in courtly manners.

All this might not have mattered had Charles felt any affection for Scotland or displayed some of his father's earthy hard-drinking and sly intelligence, which appealed to the Scots nobility, but as Angelo Correr, the Venetian envoy to London, noted after the succession, 'King James made much of the Scots while his son is close-fisted with them.' Nervous and unsure of himself, Charles could appear cold and aloof, character flaws which were heartily disliked by the Scots, who mistook his formal public manner for rudeness. It was not until July 1628 that the King gave any hint that he would travel to Edinburgh to be crowned and in the period that had passed since his accession the rumour had grown that, far from wanting to travel to Scotland, Charles had insisted that the Scottish crown should be brought to him in London. The rumours were untrue but they were believed and it was to be another five years before Charles made the journey to Edinburgh to be crowned in the bleak confines of Holyrood Abbey which had been carefully spruced up for the occasion.

In fact, from the moment he entered the city through the West Port on 15 June 1633 Edinburgh was *en fête*. The nymph Edina welcomed the King with the presentation of the keys, and the Lord Provost and his councillors, clad in scarlet, were on hand to lead the royal retinue down the lavishly decorated main street, now known as the Royal Mile, towards the Royal Palace of Holyroodhouse. The elaborate and expensive pageantry was matched by the pomp and solemnity of the crowning of Charles two days later, which was organised by the Lord Lyon King of Arms, who was moved to say that it was 'the most glorious and magnifique coronation that was ever seen in this kingdom'. Perhaps it was too gaudily done for, far from assuaging everyone's feelings, the coronation ceremony seemed to contain too many elements which were deemed to be 'popish'. The service was conducted by Archbishop Spottiswood, and the Bishop of Brechin delivered the sermon, but both these pre-eminent church leaders were obliged to wear English vestments, and the proceedings, which lasted four hours, seemed to be more Anglican than Presbyterian in nature. The Aberdeen chronicler John Spalding noted with some distaste that the altar had been covered with 'a rich tapestry wherein the crucifix was curiously wrought; and as these bishops who were in service passed by this crucifix they were seen to bow their knee and beck, which, with their habit, was noticed, and bred great fear of inbringing of Popery'.

From the very outset of its existence Hepburn's new regiment had connections not just with the British royal family but also with the House of Stewart, the Scottish royal house since 1371 when Robert II came to the throne of Scotland. All this mattered because the regiment's first experience of war was not in Charles's service but in the service of Louis XIII of France. It was not a unique arrangement: the men whom Hepburn began recruiting in the year of Charles I's Scottish coronation were following an old tradition, fighting as mercenaries in European wars in French, Danish, Swedish or Spanish service. To them, war was a lucrative national industry which had the added bonus that it could be exported. Scots made good fighters and in common with many other minorities on Europe's fringes – the Croat cavalry in Count Wallenstein's imperial army, for example – they exported their skills to the highest bidder, becoming soldiers of fortune who gave good value for money. During the Thirty Years War, which was still being fought at the time of the foundation of The Royal Scots, at least 25,000 Scots were in the service of Gustavus Adolphus of Sweden, while half as many fought for King Louis XIII of France, often confronting their fellow countrymen on the field of battle, neither giving quarter nor expecting to receive it. The experience of fighting in foreign service had begun 200 years earlier when John Stewart of Darnley led a Scots army which fought for the French in their perennial wars against England (known to history as the Hundred Years War) and as a result a *Garde Ecossaise* came into being, with the Stewarts, by then ennobled as Lords of Aubigny, as their hereditary commanders. Their 'high military reputation' was confirmed by chroniclers such as Henry Torrens and Jean Froissart, who spoke of them as 'bold, hardy and much inured to war in a national sense' and later, in the nineteenth century, the novelist Sir Walter Scott wrote admiringly of them in his novels *Quentin Durward* and *The Legend of Montrose*. Scott also wrote his own tribute in words which get to the heart of the matter by explaining the reasons for the love of soldiering abroad entertained by his fellow countrymen:

> The contempt of commerce entertained by young men having some pretence to gentility, the poverty of the country of Scotland, the national disposition to wandering and to adventure, all conduced to lead the Scots abroad into the military service of countries that were at war with each other.

The pattern continued throughout the sixteenth century and into the seventeenth, when the outbreak of the Thirty Years War created a fresh demand for soldiers that the Scots were able to exploit. (The war was fought between 1618 and 1648 between Europe's Protestant powers, backed by Catholic France, to contain the territorial ambitions of the Habsburgs.) During its course, the regimental rolls of the Swedish army were thick with the names of Scots who served as officers and regimental commanders. Amongst them was Hepburn, who entered Swedish service as a colonel in 1625. The son of a modest East Lothian landowner, he had left Scotland as a young man following a desultory education at St Andrews and had experience of fighting in Bohemia and the Netherlands before offering his sword to Gustavus Adolphus, the greatest of the Protestant military leaders. During the fighting in Prussia and Poland Hepburn distinguished himself as a tough fighting soldier, and after being knighted he became commander of Gustavus's 'Green Brigade', which, in addition to his own regiment, contained a number of other Scottish formations including Mackay's Highlanders, raised earlier in the war by Sir Donald Mackay, another notable Scottish soldier of fortune.

The high-water mark of their contribution came outside the village of Breitenfeld, north of Leipzig, on 18 September 1631, when the Protestant army crushed the imperial forces led by the previously invincible Count Tilly in a dazzling victory. Suddenly it seemed that the threat of Catholic domination was at an end, that never again would the Protestant Germans have cause to fear the Habsburg armies which had laid waste to their country for so many unhappy years. Their celebrations were not misplaced, for this 'first great test and trial of the new tactics against the old, and therefore the first great land battle of the modern age', had introduced new and terrifying tactics to the battlefield. Gustavus Adolphus's army won because its mobile columns and concentrated firepower were too much for the cumbersome, static and well-drilled lines of the imperial army. Breitenfeld was a declaration: the ponderous, slow-moving masses of imperial cavalry and infantry which had crushed their opposition underfoot could be defeated by the flexibility and firepower of manoeuvrable horsemen armed with matchlock pistols which were discharged at the gallop and usually at point-blank range.

Although the Swedish victory rattled the Habsburg cause it did not break it. In the following year Gustavus Adolphus hoped to reach Vienna but was forced to protect his rear from Wallenstein, now intent on forcing a battle which both men knew would be decisive. Displaying his usual recklessness, Gustavus Adolphus once had his horse shot from under him and when rebuked by his courtiers he responded that there was no sense in keeping him in a box. His optimism seemed to be rewarded by further success. Tilly was mortally wounded at the River Lech and the

Bavarian cities of Augsburg and Munich were soon in Swedish hands. Then, with winter fast approaching, came the fateful confrontation at Lützen.

Knowing that Wallenstein had been weakened by the absence of his main cavalry force under the command of Count Pappenheim, Gustavus Adolphus determined to press home the advantage, using the tactics that had served his army so well. This time, though, Wallenstein was waiting for him, with his musketeers hidden in a long ditch from which they could shoot upwards as the attacking Swedish cavalry charged over them. With his overstretched forces lined up in traditional formation, the cavalry on the wings, the infantry in the centre, he waited to receive the Swedish assault. In the hard-fought struggle which followed, the Swedish brigades succeeded in breaking the imperial line but amidst the smoke and confusion Gustavus Adolphus was fatally wounded while encouraging his men forward. The battle ended in a close-quarter struggle that left the Swedes victorious, but at a dreadful cost.

As the news of the King's death filtered back through his army's rank and file in small shockwaves of grief, men hardened by battle had difficulty fighting back their tears. For the Swedes it was a hammer blow. Gustavus Adolphus was their beloved ruler, the Lion of the North, the defender of the Protestant faith, a latter-day Gideon with seven armies and eighty thousand men under his command. For the others in his army, a curious collection of soldiers of fortune – English, German, Irish and Scots – the loss was equally grievous. He was their patron, a god of battles whom they knew to be fearless and resolute, a commander who had scattered the imperial forces of his previously invincible opponents: in the words of another Scots mercenary, Robert Monro, he was 'the King of Captains and the Captain of Kings . . . Illustrissimus amongst Generals'. However, Hepburn was not amongst the mourners. Once trusted as one of the bravest of Gustavus's brigade commanders, he had lost the confidence of the Swedish King prior to Lützen and had departed his camp with the reproachful words: 'And now sire never more shall this sword be drawn in your service; this is the last time I will ever serve so ungrateful a prince!' Ironically, the Scottish contingent was held in reserve during the battle, the first time it had not been in the vanguard during the entire campaign in southern Germany.

The Swedish loss was to be France's gain and led to the moment when The Royal Scots came into being, crossing over to France in the late summer of 1633. Serving as *Le Regiment de Hebron* it took part in the fighting in the Netherlands and Germany against Habsburg forces and it soon added to its complement other Scots who had been fighting for the Protestant cause elsewhere in Europe. Respected by the French as 'good soldiers and mostly gentlemen' they were hardy characters; they had to be, because the campaigning took them over long miles and the fighting was ruthless, with few prisoners taken and privation and death constant companions. In that respect they were probably little different from any soldier down the ages who has faced the hellish fear and shock of battle as well as the tedium and discomfort of life in the field. Contemporary records are sparse, but in 1700 Daniel Defoe produced a historical romance, *Memoirs of a Cavalier*, 'by Col. Andrew Newport' which contains a telling description of the kind of men who served in Scottish regiments such as Hepburn's:

> I confess the [Scottish] soldiers made a very uncouth figure, especially the Highlanders, the oddness and barbarity of their arms seemed to have in it something remarkable. They were generally tall swinging fellows; their swords were extravagantly, and I think significantly

broad, and they carried great wooden targets [targes, or shields], large enough to cover the upper parts of their bodies. Their dress was as antique as the rest; a cap on their heads, called by them a bonnet, long hanging sleeves behind, and their doublets, breeches, and stockings of a stuff they called plaid, striped across red and yellow, with short socks of the same. There were three or four thousand of these in the Scots army, armed only with swords and targets; and in their belts some of them had a pistol, but no muskets at that time amongst them.

In 1636 Hepburn was appointed a Marshal of France, but by then his luck was running out and the long years of campaigning were taking their toll. Having survived the opening rounds of the siege of Saverne in June, when his regiment played a leading role in the assault, he was shot in the head and died of his wounds. He was buried in the cathedral of Toul and his death was widely mourned, not least by Cardinal Richelieu, the Prime Minister of France and the guiding light behind his country's foreign policy. 'I cannot express how much I am affected by the death of poor Colonel Hepburn,' he wrote, 'not only because of the great esteem in which I held him, but also for the great zeal and devotion which he had always shown in the service of His Majesty. His loss has so pained me that I cannot be consoled.' Hepburn was succeeded by his nephew George, who was also killed by a musket ball in an attack in the following year. The colonelcy then passed to Lord James Douglas and remained in that family for many years.

Hepburn's regiment remained in French service until the end of the Thirty Years War in 1648, when the bloodletting in Europe was finally brought to an end by the Treaty of Westphalia, although it would take another six years for the great armies to be withdrawn from the main campaigning areas. In the final phases of the war the regiment fought in northern Italy against Habsburg forces, and it was during that period that the nickname of Pontius Pilate's Bodyguard seems to have come into being and been adopted by the regiment in honour of its longevity. Several versions of the story exist but the most likely version is found in Lieutenant-Colonel Robert H. Paterson's history of the regiment. The story might be apocryphal, but the origin of the nickname seems to have arisen as a result of an altercation between Hepburn's men and the French Regiment of Picardy over the right of precedent – by long-standing military tradition the senior regiment always stands on the right of the line. While the two regiments were serving together an officer in the Picardy Regiment used the nickname as an insult and added for good measure that the Scots must have been asleep at their posts while guarding Christ's body after the crucifixion. 'You must be mistaken, sir,' retorted a Scots officer, 'for had we really been the Guards of Pontius Pilate and done duty at the sepulchre, the Holy Body had never left it.'

Despite the return to peace there was no let-up in activity for Hepburn's regiment. They were involved in the continued fighting with Spain and helped to quell civil unrest in the *Fronde*, a struggle between the French Prime Minister, Cardinal Mazarin, and the *parlement* of Paris over taxation for the war effort, which had erupted in the summer of 1648. With insurrection in the air – the parlement was supported by a number of disaffected nobles and by some provincial leaders – Mazarin was sufficiently alarmed by events to threaten to use the army to blockade the capital. Denounced by the parlement as a 'disturber of the public peace, enemy of the king and his state', Mazarin was convinced that he might be sacrificed and that the future of the monarchy was at stake. In March 1649 a truce was patched up only for unrest to break out again three years later, but it too faltered, due to the lack of any unified opposition. Later, once the unrest of 1648 and

1652 was sufficiently far away, it became known as the *Fronde* after a Parisian children's street game, as if by giving it a safe name its importance was diminished.

The regiment was also involved in France's continuing war with Spain, and in 1657 was fighting alongside English troops when Oliver Cromwell's Protectorate sent 6,000 troops to join the French army in Flanders under Vicomte de Turenne. In return England would take possession of the ports of Dunkirk and Mardyke, possessions which would provide a foothold in continental Europe and hit hard at Spanish power and authority. The decisive point in the campaign was a hard-fought battle outside Dunkirk on 14 June 1658. Known as the Battle of the Dunes, the New Model Army regiments were commanded by a Scot, Sir William Lockhart of Lee, another mercenary soldier, and they were central to Turenne's victory. Ordered to attack the Spanish right, they made their assault over the sandy terrain while the English warships offered covering fire offshore. At the same time, the French infantry assaulted the centre while their horse attacked on the flanks. Under sustained pressure, the Spanish infantry was pushed back and finally broke after their cavalry fled from the field. As a battle it was all over in four hours and their army was easily routed, although some Spanish commanders, notably the Duke of York (Charles II's brother), tried to rally their men. Again, the news sent a shockwave through Europe: the Spanish were supposed to possess the world's best infantry soldiers, yet they had succumbed to the professionalism of the New Model Army and the leadership of Turenne. English losses were around a hundred, a quarter of those suffered by Turenne's army, while the Spanish lost over a thousand men as well as a good deal of military pride. Ten days later Dunkirk surrendered to Lockhart and the English moved in to take possession of the town and its vital port. For the first time since Calais was lost in 1558 the English were back on the European mainland.

It was also a prelude to Hepburn's regiment return to Britain. Following Cromwell's death and the collapse of the Protectorate Charles II was restored to the throne in 1660, and to general rejoicing set about rebuilding his kingdom after the civil wars which had torn it apart since 1638. (Usually known as the English Civil War, it is now more accurately termed the Wars of the Three Kingdoms to take account of the part played by Scotland and Ireland.) One of the main matters to be dealt with was the demobilisation of the New Model Army, which had fought in Parliament's cause during the conflict. Not only was it no longer needed, but it was also feared and greatly unpopular because it was seen as an instrument of government. (During the Protectorate Britain had been divided up into military areas under the command of Cromwell's major-generals.) Demobilising the army was the main expense on Charles II's new exchequer. The cost of maintaining the New Model Army had been a heavy burden for the Commonwealth and Protectorate, and it proved to be no less of a charge for the Convention Parliament which came into being after the Restoration. By dint of additional taxation, though, some two-thirds of the arrears had been raised and paid and hundreds of soldiers flocked back into English society. At first it was feared that they would provide a locus for troublemaking but that concern proved to be groundless: thanks to a ruthless purge of potential troublemakers in the run-up to the Restoration most of the demobbed soldiers were simply trained men who wanted to get back to their civilian lives and occupations. The payment of arrears helped, and within three years the diarist Samuel Pepys noted in conversation with his colleague, Robert Blackeburne, that the retired soldiers were the 'most substantial sort of people, and the soberest':

Of all the old army now, you cannot see a man begging about the street. But what? You shall see this Captain turned a shoemaker; the lieutenant, a Baker; this, a brewer; that, a haberdasher; this common soldier, a porter; and every man in his apron and frock, & c., as if they had never done anything else – whereas the [Royalists] go with their belts and swords, swearing and cursing and stealing – running into people's houses, by force oftentimes.

The process had been orderly, much to most people's surprise, but the reduction in the size of the army did not mean the complete demilitarisation of the three kingdoms. The New Model Army had disappeared but there remained garrisons in Ireland and Scotland, and in Dunkirk and Mardyke. All were kept in existence. Around 7,500 soldiers comprised the Restoration army in Ireland, and it was officered mainly by former New Model Army officers who had gained land in the country; only later, in the following reign, would its complexion be changed as Catholics were promoted to key posts. In Scotland the size of the army was reduced dramatically, to some 2,200 men, consisting of two regiments of foot and a troop of horse, but the changes also allowed the formation of regiments which survive to this day. A regiment of foot guards consisting of five companies was formed in 1662, and in time (1678) it became the Scots Guards, while Hepburn's regiment, now known as the *Regiment de Douglas* after the new colonel, was brought home from France to help with internal security duties in 1661 and between 1665 and 1667. The garrison in Dunkirk and Mardyke numbered 6,600. It consisted of an amalgamation of Royalists and New Model Army and it could have caused trouble but for the acquisition of Tangier in 1662, following Charles II's marriage to Catherine de Braganza of Portugal. Under the settlement Britain received the North African port as well as Bombay in India, and amongst the forces sent to Tangier from Dunkirk were one regiment of horse (later to become The Royal Dragoons) and one regiment of foot (later to become The Queen's Royal West Surrey Regiment). As for Dunkirk, it was sold to the French in October that year. Even before Charles II had dealt with the garrisons outside England, he and his first minister, the Earl of Clarendon, had decided that the King needed a personal life guard, a small force which would owe its loyalty to the Crown – Charles had seen how his father had been weakened by the lack of a reliable force. As a result, a regiment of foot guards was formed in November under the command of Colonel John Russell; known as The First Foot Guards, it later became The Grenadier Guards and, together with Le Regiment de Douglas, one of its first duties was to put down an attempted Fifth Monarchist insurrection in 1661. Led by a wine cooper called John Venner who believed that Christ's return was imminent, about 50 of his followers, including a woman dressed in armour, marched to Westminster Hall on 6 January 1661 to try to recover the heads of the regicides who had been executed shortly after Charles II had returned to the throne. The part-time militia forces in London were hard pressed to deal with the situation and in the aftermath parliament agreed to the formation of more guards regiments. In a symbolic move on 14 February 1661, General George Monck's regiment laid down its arms on Tower Hill and immediately took them up again to be reconstituted as The Lord General's Regiment of Foot in the service of the Crown; thus was born the regiment which lives on in the British Army as The Coldstream Guards. Two regiments of horse guards were added: the Duke of York's and the Duke of Albemarle's Life Guards and the Earl of Oxford's regiment, formed largely out of Cromwell's old Life Guard of Horse, the renowned 'Lobsters' formerly commanded by Sir Arthur Hesilrige. Later, this regiment would become The Royal Horse

Guards or the 'Blues' (from the colour of the uniform). Britain might have been demilitarised, in that the much-disliked New Model Army had been disbanded, but Charles now had 7,000 loyal soldiers at his disposal and in those regiments the modern British Army can trace its origins. At the time they were known not as the army but as the King's 'guards and garrisons'.

The home army was the servant of the King; he was its head – its commander was Monck, now ennobled as the Duke of Albemarle in the rank of Lord General – and it was counted as part of his household, hence its size was limited. Overseas Charles also had substantial forces on which he could call. A British brigade, under the command of Earl Inchiquin, served in the Portuguese War of Independence from 1662 to 1668, several regiments remained in French service, a joint Anglo-Scottish brigade was on loan to the Stadtholder of the United Provinces, and until Tangier was abandoned in 1684, its garrison was also available to the King. In addition to those regulars, by virtue of 'An Act declaring the sole right of the Militia to be in the King', he also had control of the militia through the lords lieutenant of the counties. All those soldiers provided Charles II with a military resource which his father had never enjoyed. The country might have been weary of the presence of the army, but Charles and his supporters were determined that the Crown should be protected by fully equipped and fully manned security forces.

Amongst them was Douglas's regiment, which made its final return to the service of the British Crown in the summer of 1678, when it became known as Dumbarton's Regiment following the ennoblement of its colonel, Lord George Douglas, as Earl of Dumbarton. After spending the winter in East Anglia it crossed over to Ireland, the first of many occasions when The Royal Scots would find themselves garrisoned in that country. Their next destination was Tangier, where the British presence had excited the opposition of the local population and fighting had broken out with the Moors under the command of the Alcaide of Alcazar. The Scots were sent to strengthen the garrison in the spring of 1680 and were destined to stay in Tangier until it was eventually abandoned in 1684, when the government decided that the costs of maintaining Charles II's dowry were not worth the outlay of money and men's lives. They were soon in action. On 14 May the Moors blew up Fort Henrietta and the British were forced to withdraw from the outlying defences – a series of forts – back towards their inner defensive lines. Despite naval support the British losses were high – the Scots lost one officer and fifteen men, killed during a disastrous day's fighting.

Tangier was not a happy posting for the fledgling British Army. In addition to facing the danger of attack by the Moors, hygiene was poor and more troops died of sickness than were killed in battle. Food was poor but alcohol was abundant, with obvious deleterious results. Pay was usually late, leave was non-existent and there were few local pleasures other than disease-ridden local women. On a visit to Tangier Samuel Pepys, the secretary for the navy, found an absence of discipline and amongst the soldiers nothing but 'swearing, cursing, drinking and whoring'. For most British soldiers sent to Tangier the posting was as bad as a death sentence. However, like all military experiences, it was not wholly bad. Dumbarton's Regiment was given its first experience of serving outside Europe in British service and the part it played in the fighting against the Moors earned the regiment its first battle honour, 'Tangier 1680'. The posting also provides the first evidence that the regiment employed its own pipers – contemporary papers show a group of kilted pipers playing on the Mole during the evacuation in 1684.

On their return the regiment was quartered in the south of

England, and it was at this time that it received from the King the title of 'The Royal Regiment of Foot'. Although it was still known as Dumbarton's Regiment in honour of its colonel, its new designation made it the senior line infantry regiment in the British Army and the first to receive a Royal title. During this period the regiment consisted of around 2,500 men contained in 21 companies all under the operational command of a lieutenant-colonel with a major and an adjutant on his headquarters staff. In every other respect the regiment was more or less owned by its colonel, who was responsible for all funds allotted by the government for clothing, equipping and paying his men. In 1697 a private of Foot was entitled to receive one cloth coat, one pair of breeches, two cravats, two pairs of shoes, one pair of yarn stockings, one hat with band, one sash and one sword with belt. The soldiers in the ranks were entirely at the mercy of their colonel and inevitably the system was open to abuse, although not as far as Dumbarton's was concerned – it was counted a good smart regiment and won plaudits for its ceremonial duties at a royal review on Putney Heath held in October 1684. However, there were many anomalies in the system, and one of them was exposed by the regiment, thus giving it an unlooked-for and perhaps unenviable position in British military history.

Because the army had come into being in such a haphazard way, soldiers were subject to Common Law and could be tried only in a civil court. Desertion in war, for example, was counted as a felony and was liable to be punished by the death sentence, but there were no provisions for offences such as striking an officer. All that changed in March 1689 when, following the accession of William and Mary of the House of Orange, the regiment was ordered to embark for service in the Netherlands. Many of the officers in Dumbarton's were Jacobite supporters who remained loyal to the recently deposed King James II and they resented the imposition of a new colonel in the shape of Frederick, Count Schomberg. (Dumbarton, a Catholic, had gone into exile with James II.) Instead of embarking at Ipswich the regiment mutinied and marched north towards the border, intending to make its way back to Scotland. A posse of Dutch guards and dragoons was sent in pursuit and overtook The Royal Regiment near Lincoln. Fortunately, good sense prevailed and there was no bloodshed, but the mutiny left the authorities in a quandary. The Scots had not committed a civil crime and could not be punished under Common Law, but there had been a serious breach of conduct. In some confusion parliament quickly rushed through a Mutiny Act on 3 April 1689, which made legal provision 'for punishing officers and soldiers who shall mutiny or desert'. There were also clauses dealing with the billeting of troops and their pay, but the Mutiny Act was a historic breakthrough in that it finally recognised the legal existence of the army. Renewed annually (apart from ten occasions when it lapsed for periods of two years) it formed the statutory authority for the maintenance of the British Army and was not replaced until 1879 with the passing of the Army Discipline and Regulation Act.

The regiment's mutiny was quickly forgotten, other than as a historical curiosity, and The Royal Scots served with distinction in the subsequent operations in the Netherlands as part of the army of the League of Augsburg, a coalition formed by England, the United Provinces of the Netherlands, Spain and the German principalities to oppose French expansionist policies in the Netherlands. The regiment now consisted of two battalions – the 2nd battalion had come into being in 1686 – and both played their part in the fighting, the main battles being Steenkirke (1692), Landen (1693) and the Siege of Namur (1695). Although the fighting achieved nothing it brought the regiment back to its traditional campaigning grounds in Europe. In the coming years

The Royal Regiment of Foot would come to know Flanders and the Low Countries well, marching and fighting over ground with names that were to become familiar and, in time, part of the regiment's many battle honours. In one action during the Battle of Steenkirke the regiment exemplified its fighting qualities after the French captured one of the colours during the withdrawal. Seeing the colour on the other side of a hedge the new colonel, Sir Robert Douglas, charged through and killed the French soldier holding the colour before throwing it back to his men. It was a courageous gesture but it cost Douglas his life, being shot by a French marksman as he made his way back to the regiment. 'Thus the Scots commander improved upon the Roman general,' noted the regiment's *Historical Records*, 'for the brave Posthumius cast his standard in the middle of the enemy for his soldiers to retrieve; but Douglas retrieved his from the middle of the enemy without any assistance, and cast it back for his soldiers to retain.'

The records also show that the regiment was also being referred to as 'the Royals', and the name stuck.

TWO

THE EUROPEAN WARS OF SUCCESSION

Both battalions of the Royals returned to England in 1697, but it was only to be a short stay in home quarters; within four years they were back in action in Europe, fighting in the war known as the War of the Spanish Succession, which broke out in 1701. Before then, as was to happen many times later in the country's history, the army had been reduced in size to save money in the expectation of peace. Although the Royals were not affected – its two battalions remained intact – the rest of the army suffered. Following the Peace of Ryswick, which brought the fighting in the Netherlands to an end, parliament decided to disband every regiment that had been raised since 1660. Although the move was never implemented, the army was reduced to a token force of 7,000 men, and some regiments only survived as cadres. All that was to change with the threat posed by France to Britain's expanding global interests. On 16 September 1701 the exiled James II (son of Charles I) died in France and one of Louis XIV's first actions was to recognise James's son (also called James, and known as the Old Pretender) as King of Great Britain. With that move, and following Louis's claim on the throne of Spain by supporting his grandson Philip of Anjou to succeed the childless King Charles II, another war in Europe was inevitable. On the one side England, Austria and the United Provinces created a military alliance to prevent this blatant French expansionism, while on the other France and Spain combined with the assistance of the German state of Bavaria. Later Portugal and Savoy joined the French alliance.

The scene was set for over a century of armed conflict in Europe and, later, across the globe, as Britain and France vied for superiority while at the same time fighting to bring about the other's destruction. During that period the British Army was to expand dramatically and to lay the foundations for its modern existence. Between 1700 and 1800 11 new cavalry and 67 new infantry regiments came into being, while the old civilian-controlled Ordnance Board, which provided the logistics and artillery, was transmogrified to create The Royal Regiment of Artillery and the Corps of Royal Engineers. After 1751 the infantry regiments lost their colonel's names and were numbered 1st to 49th and at the height of the war in America in the 1770s the strength of the army stood at 80,579. At the same time its annual cost to the exchequer was over £3 million. While political and strategic considerations made these rapid changes inevitable, one man was responsible for turning Britain into a professional military nation with a well-trained and well-equipped regular army – John Churchill, Duke of Marlborough, the Captain-General who was hailed throughout the army as 'Corporal John' or 'the Old Corporal'. Lest that be taken as national pride speaking, the evidence of his own soldiers is enough to prove that Marlborough was regarded in his day as an outstanding field commander and that rare beast, a soldier's general. In the words of one of his soldiers, Sergeant John Millner:

> He [Marlborough] secured the affections of his soldiers
> by his good nature, care for their provisions, and vigilance
> not to expose them to unnecessary danger, and gained
> those of his officers by affability; both one and the other
> followed him to action with such a cheerfulness, resolution
> and unanimity as were sure presages of success.

Some idea of Marlborough's influence as the nation's commander-in-chief can be seen in the inexorable growth of his army during his period in command. In 1702, at the outset of war, it numbered 31,000 men; by 1706 it had increased to 50,000 and it peaked at 75,000 five years later, before declining to 23,500 in 1713 when Marlborough was no longer in favour. There were also changes in arms and equipment. By the beginning of the new century the pike had all but disappeared as an infantry weapon and the old matchlock muskets were being replaced by the flintlock musket, which was capable of firing two rounds a minute. With its plug bayonet the flintlock was a formidable weapon, but it had to be used properly and with the utmost discipline. Twenty-one words of command were needed to prime, load and fire the weapon, and as a result infantry regiments put much effort into weapon training and the close-order drills which were necessary to manoeuvre regiments on the battlefield. Once in action regiments formed up and fought in exactly the same patterns as they practised on the parade ground, and close-order drill was regarded not just as a means of disciplining the men but also of ensuring their survival in combat.

The Royals joined Marlborough's army in the summer of 1701 and they were destined to serve under him at his great victories of Blenheim, Ramillies, Oudenarde and Malplaquet, names which are indelibly linked with the British Army and which form an important part of the Royals' collection of battle honours. With reinforcements, including the addition of two new companies of grenadiers, the Royals had a complement of around 2,000 men by the time that Marlborough opened his campaign. (The grenadiers were specialist troops, usually tall men dressed in distinctive conical caps, who were the regiment's bombers.) The regiment also had a new colonel in Lord George Hamilton, who had been created Earl of Orkney in 1696 – as a result they are often referred to as 'Orkney's' in Marlborough's order of battle. Hamilton, a scion of the Douglas and Angus families, had joined the army as a youngster and went on to become one of Marlborough's most able field commanders. In 1736, a year before his death, he became the British Army's first field marshal.

In the opening stages of the conflict the fighting was restricted to the Low Countries, but Marlborough was determined to take the war into Germany and to put pressure on the Bavarian army of the Elector Maximilian Emmanuel, which was threatening Vienna while Austrian forces were fighting in north Italy. At first Marlborough hoped to do this by moving his army into the valley of the Moselle, but it soon became evident that he would have to go further south and march to the Danube to prevent the French forces, under Marshal Tallard, from meeting up with the Bavarians. To do that he would have to take the coalition army, numbering 40,000 (soon to be 60,000 as other units joined) complete with artillery, stores and horses, over a distance of 250 miles, an operation which required a massive amount of organisation and forethought on the part of Marlborough and his staff. The Captain-General explained his thinking in a letter to his Quartermaster-General, Colonel William Cadogan (later General, 1st Earl Cadogan, a distinguished soldier):

> You do well apprehend that good order and military discipline are the chief essentials in an army. But you must be ever aware that an army cannot preserve good

order unless its soldiers have meat in their bellies, coats on their backs, and shoes on their feet. All these are as necessary as arms and munitions. I pray you to look to these things as you may do to the other matters.

Marlborough's advice was offered in December 1703, following Cadogan's appointment to his army, but any soldier from any age will recognise the universal truth of the sentiments contained in that letter.

The Royals began their long march south on 27 April and, like everyone else in Marlborough's army, bar the high command, they were kept in the dark about their final destination. Marching at an average of 12 miles a day, with every fourth day a rest day, they made good progress, and by the end of June they had made contact with the Austrian army under the command of Prince Eugene of Savoy, to the north of Ulm. On the way they had been joined by other allies, Hanoverians and Danes, and as Captain Robert Parker, 18th Foot, recorded in his diaries, the operation had been perfectly planned from start to finish:

> As we marched through the countries of our allies, Commissaries were appointed to furnish us with all manner of necessaries for men and horse; these were brought to the ground before we arrived, and the soldiers had nothing to do, but pitch their tents, boil their kettles, and lie down to rest. Surely never was such a march carried on with more order and regularity and with less fatigue, both to man and horse.

And to continue Parker's thinking, never before had an army moved across such a huge distance with so little disruption to the local population and with so little cost to itself – fewer than

1,000 men were lost to desertion during the course of the march, a remarkable achievement considering the terrain and the length of the ground covered. The trick now was to take advantage of surprise and to attack the enemy before Tallard's French forces, advancing from the Rhine, joined the Bavarian army which was deployed north of Augsburg along the Danube. The first action took place on 2 July on the heights of Schellenberg 500 feet above the Danube, a commanding position which guarded the approaches to the fortifications at Donauworth. To avoid flanking fire, Marlborough decided to attack the Bavarian positions where they were strongest. The main assault column numbered 6,000 soldiers and both battalions of the Royals took part in the main attack as part of the advance guard, fighting in the same brigade as the 1st (Grenadier) Guards. The Battle of Schellenberg was marked by close-quarter fighting and it resulted in an inevitably high casualty count. Of the British casualties of 29 officers and 407 soldiers killed and 86 officers and 1,031 soldiers wounded the Royals lost proportionately. The 1st battalion had 3 officers and 39 soldiers killed plus 10 officers and 106 soldiers wounded. Losses in the 2nd battalion were 2 officers and 74 soldiers killed and 15 officers and 196 soldiers wounded. It was, though, a battle well worth winning, as it provided a safe crossing of the Danube and inflicted an early defeat on the opposition before Tallard could intervene with his reinforcements from Landau. A watching French officer, Colonel Jean de la Colonie, later wrote a vivid eye-witness account of the storming of his defences which gives some idea of the conditions facing the Royals when they went into the attack:

> The English [*sic*] infantry led this attack with the greatest
> intrepidity, right up to our parapet, but they were opposed
> with a courage at least equal to their own. Rage, fury and

desperation were manifested by both sides, with the more obstinacy as the assailants and assailed were perhaps the bravest soldiers in the world. The little parapet which separated the two forces became the scene of the bloodiest struggle that could be conceived . . . It would be impossible to describe in words strong enough the details of the carnage that took place during this first attack, which lasted a good hour or more. We were all fighting hand to hand, hurling them back as they clutched at the parapet; men were slaying, or tearing at the muzzles of the guns and the bayonets which pierced their entrails, crushing under their feet their own wounded comrades, and even gouging out their opponents' eyes with their nails, when the grip was so great that neither could make use of their weapons.

Schellenberg has often been overlooked by the historians, but by inflicting an early defeat on the enemy and securing the Danube crossing Marlborough paved the way for his great victory at Blenheim.

A month later, following a game of cat-and-mouse in which Maximilian Emmanuel refused battle until he received reinforcements, Tallard's French army eventually joined forces with the Bavarians. In an attempt to force the issue by provoking the enemy Marlborough had destroyed hundreds of Bavarian villages, but it proved to be a futile exercise. On 10 August, Marlborough received a message from the commander of the Austrian forces, Prince Eugene of Savoy, informing him that he had made contact with the opposition, and the two forces met near the villages of Blindheim (Blenheim) and Oberglau on the confluence of the rivers Nebel and Danube. Both sides were evenly balanced in terms of men (some 55,000 apiece) and guns, but Tallard was taken by surprise and was forced to take up an inferior position, with the Danube on his right flank. The plan was that Marlborough's forces would attack the French on the enemy right while Eugene would deal with the Bavarians, who were drawn up on the French left. The battle began shortly after mid-day on 13 August when the British left, under Lord John Cutts, a force of some 20 battalions including 2nd Royal Scots, attacked towards Blenheim while Marlborough moved towards the centre at Oberglau. At the same time Eugene took on Maximilian's forces in a hard-hitting assault which prevented them from coming to the assistance of the French.

Once across the Nebel, which ran across the battlefield, Marlborough's force, including 1st Royal Scots, lined itself up in a new formation with two lines of infantry protected by two lines of cavalry, and by the end of the afternoon, shortly after half past five, Tallard's centre had been breached and the battle was as good as over. It was a brilliant victory. The French army had been decisively beaten and on the allied right the Bavarians broke under pressure from Eugene and began streaming away from the battlefield. Many of those fleeing were drowned in the Danube and, overall, the losses on the French and Bavarian side spoke only of a terrible defeat – 38,600 killed, wounded or taken prisoner. Amongst them was Tallard, who became a prisoner. In his official report of the battle Marlborough was quick to praise those who had done the fighting – 'the bravery of all our troops on this occasion cannot be expressed, the Generals, as well as the officers and soldiers, behaving themselves with the greatest courage and resolution' – but the battle was also a model of coalition warfare in which the two allied commanders, Marlborough and Eugene, had acted in perfect harmony to secure one of the greatest British victories over the French since Agincourt, three centuries earlier.

After the battle Marlborough's army returned to the Low

Countries and, with the rest of the British Army, the Royals enjoyed a well-earned period of rest and recuperation. Under a special dispensation, all officers and men of the Royals received special bounties from the government, an indication of the country's growing reliance on its armed forces. Following the excitements of Blenheim, the next year was something of an anticlimax, but between then and 1709 the Royals were to be involved in Marlborough's next three victories, which helped to pave the way to a successful conclusion of the conflict at the Treaty of Utrecht in April 1713. These battles and the supporting operations were fought over Flanders, Ghent and Picardy – ground which would be indelibly associated with the history of the British Army in the years to come. The second of Marlborough's great victories was fought at Ramillies, to the north of Namur, on 23 May, where the joint French–Bavarian armies were under the command of Marshal Villery and Maximilian Emmanuel. Although victory owed something to luck, in that Marlborough came across the enemy forces as they were manoeuvring into position, he took advantage of the surprise by immediately attacking the centre, using his coalition forces to assault the enemy lines while deploying his British regiments to threaten the French left. Overwhelmed, the enemy broke and the combat phase of the battle was over within hours, with the French and Bavarians losing around 15,000 casualties and the coalition one-third of that number. As a result of the victory the Spanish Netherlands was cleared of enemy forces.

The following year saw France and her allies go on the offensive, with the intention of retrieving lost ground in Flanders and preparing the way for a planned invasion of England, using Antwerp as a jumping-off point. For a short time in April the Royals were earmarked as part of a small force which would be returned to England to counter the danger, but following a short and uncomfortable period aboard ship they were returned to Ghent in time for the new campaigning season. Oudenarde, to the south of Ghent, was fought on 11 July 1708, and the Royals took part in the second phase of the attack, serving in a division of infantry commanded by the Duke of Argyll. As happened so often in Marlborough's battles, the outcome depended on the infantry's ability to stand firm in the face of close-quarter fire and bayonet charges before the cavalry attacked to roll up the opposition flanks. When the French finally broke, pursuit proved to be impossible in the failing light, with the result that they were given the opportunity to retreat in reasonably good order towards Ghent. In the next stage of operations the Royals were involved in the siege of Lille, which eventually fell at the beginning of December. During that year the Royals were also deployed in the forces which prevented the Bavarians from besieging Brussels, and the year ended with the regiment going into winter quarters at Ghent.

Malplaquet, the fourth of Marlborough's victories, was fought on 11 September 1709 and it proved to be the toughest of the quartet. It was fought to the south of Mons, where the French under Villars occupied a well-defended position on wooded rising ground. Once again, the Royals formed part of the force which would attack the centre, under Orkney's overall command, while the cavalry attacked the flanks. This time the French offered stouter opposition and the infantry was hard pressed to steady the line as the cavalry regrouped. Later, one of Marlborough's officers remembered that the defeat of the French was won at a heavy cost – 'a deluge of blood was spilt to dislodge them'. French casualties were estimated at around 14,000. The Royals' losses were put at one officer and seventy-one soldiers killed or wounded. War-weariness gradually crept into the conflict, and after Malplaquet the Royals were involved in a series of sieges of the major garrisons in the Spanish Netherlands while diplomatic moves were instigated to broker a peace settlement. At the beginning of 1712 Marlborough was replaced by the Duke of Ormond and the resultant peace negotiations at Utrecht brought the fighting to an end. Philip was acknowledged as King of Spain and the Protestant succession was recognised in Britain, but the lasting legacy of the war was the recognition that a balance of power in Europe would take precedence over dynastic rights in the negotiation of future European affairs. That outcome and the emergence of Britain as a major power owed everything to Marlborough's generalship and the abilities and professionalism of the British Army. In 1714 the Royals' two battalions returned to Britain, where they were garrisoned on the south coast before crossing over to Ireland for a peacetime deployment which would last the best part of a quarter of a century. (They had already experienced service in Ireland for a short period in the 1690s.)

From contemporary evidence it is clear that the Royals recruited from a wide variety of backgrounds and needed a constant stream of drafts to keep them up to strength. Most continued to come from Scotland but the years in Ireland also produced recruits from British settlers in Ireland (only later, after 1771, were Catholics allowed to enlist), a trend which continued in the next century, with many of the contemporary recruiting songs being common to both countries:

> Courage, boys, 'tis one to ten,
> But we return all gentlemen
> All gentlemen as well as they,
> Over the hills and far away.
> Over the hills and o'er the Main,
> To Flanders, Portugal and Spain,
> The Queen commands and we'll obey
> Over the hills and far away . . .

Officers tended to come from the wealthier sections of society and were supposed to have private incomes to maintain their standards of living and to keep at least one servant who would prepare or purchase his meals and deal with the demands of entertainment. Uniform also set the officers apart. It was their responsibility to look the part and to make sure that they had sufficient changes of clothing in their baggage to impress visitors or allied officers and to retain their own status within the regiment. In the Royals an officer wore a red coat with blue facings, a sash at waist level with a knotted and tasselled end and a neck cloth on which sat a silver gorget, which signified his rank. All officers wore wigs, but by the time of Marlborough's campaigns these had become less flamboyant and the smaller 'campaign wig' was in general use. The hat had its brim turned up on three sides and was trimmed with silver braid, gauntlets were made of leather and boots or buckled shoes were worn with grey stockings. Ever concerned about saving costs, Marlborough insisted that all the soldiers in his army should 'make do and mend', and it was not unusual for the effects of dead soldiers to be passed around the regiment for use by the needier soldiers.

Inspection of the regiment's rolls reveals that the Royals' officers conformed to the type found throughout Marlborough's army. All were reasonably well off, some owned land or were heirs to estates and most were well connected. However, that does not tell the whole story about the social mix within the regiment. Some of the rank and file had a good conceit of themselves and either came from modest farming backgrounds or used their experience in the army to better themselves. One of the latter was Donald McBane (or McBain), who served with the Royals in Marlborough's campaigns and wrote an entertaining account of his experiences in a spirited book entitled *The Expert Sword-man's Companion; or the True Art of Self-Defence, With all Account of the Author's Life and*

his Transactions during the Wars with France, to which is annexed,
The Arts of Gunnerie, Illustrated with 22 etched copper plates, which
was published in Glasgow in 1728. A native of Inverness, McBane
first joined the Royals in 1695, but his attachment to the regiment
was highly irregular and at one time he found himself serving
in the Earl of Angus's 26th Regiment. From an early age he had
been interested in the art of swordsmanship, an interest that was
fuelled by his involvement in several duels as a younger man, and
while serving in Flanders he seems to have been permitted to run
a fencing school in his spare time. As his memoirs make clear, he
was allowed to continue even when the regiment was on campaign
in Flanders:

> I continued keeping my School. A short Time after I
> came to know that there was Four good Swords men in
> the Town that kept Women and Gaming, the Wheel of
> Fortune and *Ledgerdemain* [card tricks] by which they got
> vast Money. I resolved to have a share of that Gain, at least
> to have a fair Tryall for it. I Fought all the Four, one by
> one; the last of them was Lefthanded; he and I went to the
> Rampart where we searched one another for Fire Arms.
> Finding none, we drew and had two or three clean Turns:
> at last he put up his Hand and took a Pistol from the Cock
> of his Hat; he cocked it against his shoulder and presented
> it to me, upon which I asked Quarters, but he refused,
> calling me an 'English Bouger', and Fired at me and ran
> for it. One of the balls went through my Cravat . . . at last
> I overtook him over against the Guard and gave him a
> Thrust in the Buttocks; then I fled to the Fleshmarket;
> nobody could take me out there, it being a Priviledged
> Place. I tarried there till Night, then went Home to my
> Quarters and called for his Commerads that same Night,

who agreed to give me a Brace of Whoors and Two Petty
Couns a week. With this and my School I lived very well
for that Winter.

To McBane falls one other distinction. For reasons that are unclear,
even from the evidence of his autobiography, during the Battle of
Malplaquet McBane found himself looking after one of his sons
when the woman who was supposed to be caring for him went in
search of her husband. Nothing daunted, McBane put the child
in his haversack and continued fighting. Both survived the battle
despite the son receiving a wound in his right arm. As if that were
not sufficiently unusual, the Royals also had the oldest participant
in the battle – William Hiseland, who had fought in King Charles
I's civil wars and was aged 89 at the time of Malplaquet. He
continued serving with the regiment until 1713, when he retired
from the army and was admitted as an in-pensioner at the Royal
Hospital in Chelsea. This charitable institution, which still exists
today, had been founded by King Charles II in 1682 for the care
of veteran soldiers, who by the eighteenth century were wearing
their distinctive scarlet coats (blue in winter) and three-cornered
hats.

During this period, which was known as 'the long peace', the
army stagnated and, as happened so often in Britain's history,
defence expenditure was reduced and soldiers became extremely
unpopular in the public mind. Fortunately for the Royals they
escaped the worst of the problems – low morale leading to
desertions and a high crime rate – and their time in Ireland
was spent reasonably profitably, if erratically. Instead of being
concentrated on specific areas, the regiment's companies were
scattered across Ireland and the Order Books show that scarcely
any major Irish town was not garrisoned by soldiers of The Royal
Scots at one point or another. At the beginning of 1737 the Earl

of Orkney died, aged 71, and was succeeded by the Hon. James St Clair, who had joined the army as a small boy and had served as an ensign in The Royal Scots, fighting with them at Malplaquet. In common with past practice, the regiment was often listed in the order of battle as 'St Clair's' or 'Sinclair's' but following the reforms of 1751, which introduced standard numbering, he was the last colonel to be dignified in this way. Slowly the idea was being introduced that potential recruits should not be interested so much in joining the army as joining a particular regiment. Men would be drawn to a regiment by its history and exploits and in the Royals' case by its lineage in the British Army – being 'First of Foot' counted for a great deal. Being a freemason also helped – in 1732 The Royal Scots became the first regiment in the British Army to establish a Military Lodge and the practice quickly spread to other regiments.

The years of unbroken peace came to a close towards the end of the 1730s when Spain emerged as a hostile threat to British trading interests, especially in the West Indies and Caribbean, and war seemed inevitable. It was also popular, and the Royals benefited from an upsurge in recruiting, with the full establishment reaching around 1,700 officers and men in 1739. Two years later the 2nd battalion sailed to the West Indies, where it took part in Admiral Vernon's unsuccessful attack on the Spanish possession of Porto Bello in what is now modern Brazil. As was so frequently the case in operations in that part of the world, the majority of the casualties was caused not by battle but by fever and the depredations of the climate, and the Royals suffered accordingly. By the time the 2nd battalion returned to England at the end of 1742 it had sustained 90 per cent casualties. Following postings in the north of England it returned to Ireland in 1745 to regroup.

During the same period, the 1st battalion was involved in further campaigning in Europe, fighting in the war known as the War of the Austrian Succession (or King George's War). Once again, the conflict was caused by a disputed claim to a throne. At the time of his death in 1740 the Emperor Charles VI of Austria left no male heir and was succeeded by his daughter Maria Theresa. Although this possibility had been codified by the Pragmatic Sanction of 1713, a European convention which was supposed to guarantee the integrity of Maria Theresa's throne, the succession of a female ruler was opposed by Philip V of Spain, France and the electors of Bavaria and Saxony. Britain was drawn into the conflict by Prussia's decision to invade the Austrian province of Silesia – Austria was a long-standing ally – and by France's threatening moves in Flanders. In the middle of 1743 a British force including 1st Royal Scots, crossed over to Flanders under the command of King George II, but it was not in serious action until 10 May 1745. This was the Battle of Fontenoy, a hard-pounding struggle against the French where the allied forces came under the command of the Duke of Cumberland, George II's second son. It resulted in high casualties, largely due to the close-quarter combat and the ferocity of the cannonade, but, like Marlborough's battles, it proved the worth and solidity of the British infantry. Both sides lost around 7,000 casualties, killed and wounded, and the Royals' losses were proportionate – 87 killed and 191 wounded. In September the 1st battalion returned to England and was later involved in an ineffectual raid against the French bases on the Atlantic coast at L'Orient and Quiberon. The war was eventually concluded by the Treaty of Aix-la-Chapelle in 1748.

While the British Army was once again distinguishing itself in the fields of Flanders there was a sudden emergency closer to home, when the supporters of the Jacobites made a fresh claim to the British throne and put the Hanoverian succession at risk. Thirty years had passed since the last credible threat – made in 1715 by the Old Pretender – and when the rising began in the summer of 1745 it seemed that it would be no more successful. The claim was made by Prince Charles Edward Stewart (or Stuart) on behalf of his father, who would have reigned as James III, had the campaign been successful. Like so many other episodes associated with the Jacobite cause, it had a romantic beginning and a tragic ending. On 25 July 1745 Charles, or 'Bonnie Prince Charlie' as he was soon to be known, landed in the western Highlands at Moidart accompanied by seven supporters and set about the near-impossible task of encouraging the Highland clan leaders to join his father's cause. He received a mixed response. Some clan leaders supported him out of conviction and loyalty to the Stewart family: the first visible backing came from Cameron of Lochiel in Inverness-shire, who offered 700 loyal clansmen with the noble thought that, come what may, they would share the fate of their prince and leader. Others refused outright, including the Macdonalds of Sleat and the Macleods of Dunvegan, in whose lands the uprising had begun. Others hedged their bets by sending modest forces commanded by younger sons, but the sorry truth is that for all the historical romanticism engendered by the Jacobite Uprising of 1745–46 it was doomed from the start by the failure of the Highlands to give it widespread support and the unwillingness of the French to provide any credible military backing. The Lowlands were another matter: by the middle of the eighteenth century they had lost any interest in the Stewart cause and were happier to embrace the benefits provided by the 1707 Act of Union, which had joined together the parliaments of England and Scotland and laid the foundations for the modern British state.

Nevertheless Bonnie Prince Charlie enjoyed a run of early successes which bolstered optimism that his uprising might succeed, and with war raging in Europe it caused chaos and crisis in London. It helped that the government garrison in Scotland was not only weak but badly led, and by the middle of September Edinburgh was in the Prince's hands. The Jacobites' first military success came on 21 September at Prestonpans in East Lothian, where General Sir John Cope's government force was defeated and routed, having been unnerved by the speed and ferocity of the Highlanders' charge on their lines. After the battle a contemptuous song came into being, making fun of Cope's predicament – 'Hey, Johnnie Cope are ye waukin' yet?' – and it is one of the curiosities of military history that the tune is still popular in Scottish regiments as a reveille. Following that relatively easy success, Charles's army marched into England with the intention of attacking London, but they never got that far. Discouraged by the onset of winter and the growing distance from their heartlands, Highlanders began deserting or making it clear to their officers that they had no stomach for further fighting. (At that time there was usually no campaigning during the winter months.) The lack of support from English Jacobites was also disheartening and, having reached Derby, on Friday, 5 December, Charles took the fateful decision to return to Scotland.

Greatly depleted and with morale sinking, Bonnie Prince Charlie's Jacobite army began the long march back to Scotland. Even as they did so, the government had already begun preparations to crush the rebels by deploying a superior force against them under the command of the Duke of Cumberland, freshly returned from Flanders. Amongst the regiments mobilised was 2nd Royal Scots, which crossed over to Scotland in September to join an army which would eventually number 15 battalions of infantry (including the 21st, later The Royal Scots Fusiliers and the 25th, later The King's Own Scottish Borderers), the irregular Argyll Militia, 4 units of 800 mounted soldiers and a small but effective force of artillery. Despite a setback at Falkirk at the beginning of the year, Cumberland had the upper hand. Not only was his force almost twice as large as the dwindling Jacobite army, but his troops had undergone different training and were now better equipped to withstand the shock of a Highland charge. When the two armies met on the open land of Drumossie Moor, between Inverness and Nairn on 16 April 1746 on a raw early spring morning, there could only be one outcome. Most of the Prince's men showed great courage, they were outnumbered almost two to one, but they were badly led and most were tired, hungry and dispirited. In contrast Cumberland's men were confident of victory, cheering on their leader with shouts of 'Flanders, Flanders!' when he rode out to inspect them before the battle.

In keeping with their position, the Royals took the right of the front line with Cholmondeley's (34th, later The Border Regiment) to their left and they received the brunt of the charge made by Clan Chattan as they careered towards them from the Jacobite centre. The assault was soon halted by the combined fire of the artillery firing grapeshot and the steady musket fire of the infantry, as was the subsequent charge made by the Clan Macdonald. Later, men in the government army would remember the Highlanders vainly holding up their plaids against their faces as if they were facing hail instead of a storm of bullets and assorted pieces of old iron, which cut through their ranks killing and disembowelling the weary clansmen. Soon the fury of the battle slackened and, with Cumberland's cavalry committed to the battle, the Highlanders started to cast aside their weapons and run from the moor, leaving it to the smoke and the wind and the rain. Within an hour the subalterns in the Royals were telling their men to 'Rest on your Arms!', muskets were lowered and the men looked over the moor at the charnel house they had created. Even the veterans of Flanders were dumbfounded by the scene – a heaving mass of dead and dying piled up in the tufts of heather, the air thick with the moans and shrieks of the wounded. As Alexander Taylor of the

Royals put it in his memoir of the battle, his regiment had made 'a most dreadful Havock' and as a result 'there's two thousand fewer Rebels than was Yesterday Morning'.

In the aftermath of the battle the regiment took part in the mopping-up operations, a beastly business which one government officer, writing in the *London Magazine*, characterised as his men 'carrying fire and destruction as they passed, shooting the vagrant Highlanders they met in the mountains and driving off their cattle'. Unfortunately, the Royals were involved in a number of reprisals following the battle: these included the summary execution of 31 Highland officers found sheltering in the grounds of Culloden House and the sacking of the Lovat stronghold at Beauly. Atrocities of that kind were excused by the unfounded allegation that the Jacobite army had orders to kill all wounded government soldiers, and it is also true that Cumberland's commanders regarded the Highlanders as a sub-species of vicious natives, but the government army's behaviour in the months after Culloden left a dark shadow over Scottish history. It was also the beginning of a long process of subjugation of the Highlands and destruction of the Gaelic way of life, culminating in the Disarming Acts which prevented Highlanders from carrying arms or wearing Highland dress.

The Royals remained in Scotland until 1748, when they returned to Ireland, which was to be home to both battalions for the next two decades. For the regiment, and for the other English and Scottish regiments which fought against the Jacobites, it had been a curious experience. Culloden was the last battle to be fought on British soil, it was a resounding victory for the government forces and it prevented any hope of a revival in Jacobite fortunes, yet it was never recognised as a battle honour by the British Army. The battle also underlined the dreadful anomalies and divisions caused by civil war. Lord George Murray, Bonnie Prince Charlie's most trusted field commander who commanded the Jacobite right, had once held a commission in the Royals. During the charge of Clan Chattan, the Chisholms of Strathglass were led into battle by their clan chief's youngest son Roderick Og Chisholm. Facing him in the ranks of the Royals, serving in the rank of captain, were two of his brothers, James and John Chisholm. Like every other internecine war, the Jacobite Uprising pitted family against family – brother against brother, father against son – proving the adage that in civil war the winners gain their victories at a dreadful personal cost.

THREE

GLOBAL WAR: THE CONFLICTS AGAINST FRANCE AND SPAIN

In some respects the eighteenth century was the heyday of soldiering in Scotland, as thousands of Scots benefited from the expansion of Britain's growing commercial empire, which came about largely as a result of the war against the country's main continental rivals, France and Spain. To a great extent the figures speak for themselves. Between 1714 and 1763 a quarter of the officers serving in the British Army were of Scots origin, proportionally more than the English. Of 208 officers who were also members of parliament from 1750 to 1794, 56 were Scots. At the same time, one in four regimental officers in the British Army were Scots, and Scottish officers were used to receiving high command while fighting in the European and colonial wars waged by Britain throughout the eighteenth century – David Baird, one of the army's greatest generals in India, being a good example of the type. Between 1725 and 1800, no fewer than 37 Highland regiments were raised to serve in the British Army, and by the end of the period the numbers involved are estimated at 70,000 men.

There was also the opportunity to serve abroad in the army of the Honourable East India Company or in the British regiments which supported it. Many individuals enriched themselves in the process, and the history of the eighteenth-century conquest of India is littered with examples of Scots making fortunes for themselves while working in the Company's service. The opposite is also true, and countless Scots served their country with no other thought than to do their duty or lead an adventurous life in an exciting country. However, all too often, when these fortune-hunters left Scotland many forgot to take their consciences with them, leaving the poet Thomas Campbell to lament in his poem 'The Pleasures of Hope':

> Rich in the gems of India's gaudy zone,
> And plunder piled from kingdoms not their own,
> Degenerate trade! Thy minions could despise
> The heartborn anguish of a thousand cries . . .

Campbell's complaint can be given substance by many examples of Scots who left their native land to better themselves, none more so than the entrepreneur James Johnston of Westerhall, who made a fortune in India second only to the greatest 'nabob' of them all, Robert Clive (who was largely responsible for the creation of Britain's holdings in India upon the ruins of the Mogul empire). But theirs was not the whole story. The second half of the eighteenth century saw the expansion and consolidation of Britain's colonial and commercial empire in India, the Far East and North America. It could not be achieved in a single field of operations: the enterprise also meant taking on and defeating the French, not just in Europe but also at sea and in every quarter of the globe where the British and the French were in competition. The resulting conflict is known as the Seven Years War, but given its global reach and the shifting alliances it produced, it has a good claim to be referred to as the First World War.

During that time Scotland also changed. The country became increasingly urbanised and, with heavy industries taking root in the Forth and Clyde valleys, its population was centred mainly in the central belt. The long retreat from the countryside had begun, a process hastened by improving landlords who were busy cutting the old ties that bound their tenants to the land by removing them and making way for modern agrarian methods in the name of commercial development. All over Scotland, but especially in the Highland areas, people were moved off the land to make way for the husbandry of sheep and cattle; in the first instances of this depopulation they were settled on the coastal plains, but later they were encouraged to migrate, mainly to North America. For Scotland's rural population this was the end of an old way of life: not having security of tenure they had no voice in the matter, and the old social order they represented was left to wither and die.

The army, too, was changing. As we have seen, it had expanded to meet the country's strategic requirements, and this meant that regiments had to fight hard to get their allocation of recruits. The task was left in the hands of the regimental officers, although in time of war they were assisted by the civil authorities who were able to coerce men to join up under legislation provided by temporary recruiting acts. Regimental recruiting parties employed a number of blandishments to persuade young men to join their ranks. For obvious reasons, much recruiting was carried out in public houses where drink was a ready companion to tales of derring-do, and smartly dressed sergeants were only too ready to spin yarns to gullible young men. Although the army as a career was an unpopular calling, 'going for a soldier' appealed to young men who were out of work or looking for an escape from the boredom of everyday life. Men also joined the army to avoid being sent to jail or to get away from the responsibilities of an unwanted fatherhood. Inevitably, many of the candidates were physically or mentally incapable of dealing with the demands of a soldier's life, but most responsible regiments did their best to attract likely young men who would stay the course. A typical contemporary recruiting poster, issued in Glasgow in 1760, made it clear that the regiments were looking for recruits who were 'able Bodied, Sound in their limbs, free from Ruptures, Scald heads, Ulcerous sores or any remarkable deformity'. By the same token the poster made it clear that the army did not want any of the following: 'No Strollers, Vagabonds, Tinkers, Chimney Sweepers, Colliers or Saylors to be Inlisted, but such men only as were born in the Neighbourhood of the place they are inlisted in & of whom you can get and give a good Account'.

Against that background, The Royal Scots came of age in the British Army as it entered its second hundred years of service to the Crown. It was also fortunate in its postings at a time when deployments could be haphazard and in some cases downright precarious. One unfortunate regiment, the 38th Foot, was sent to the Leeward Islands in 1707, where it was promptly forgotten by the authorities in London and was not recalled to Britain until 1764. By then it had 'gone native' and a new commanding officer was shocked when he arrived in the islands to find that not only had the regiment been decimated by disease, but that the survivors had farmed out their jobs to others while the officers had abnegated all responsibility by taking on better paid civilian work. Things were better arranged in the Royals. For the first part of this period the regiment's home was Ireland, although the 1st battalion served in the final operations of the War of the Austrian Succession in 1747–48, while the 2nd battalion remained in Scotland as part of the internal peacekeeping forces in the uneasy period following the collapse of the Jacobite rebellion. At the beginning of 1748 the battalion was pulled out of the Highlands and deployed in the neighbourhood of Edinburgh and in the East Lothian towns of Dunbar, Haddington, Musselburgh and Prestonpans. Later, this was considered to be an integral part of the regiment's traditional recruiting area and the towns concerned all laid down strong connections with The Royal Scots.

The first sign of imminent change came in December 1756 when the 2nd battalion was named as part of a force of eight regiments sent to reinforce the garrison in North America. To get up to the required strength of 1,154 soldiers, the battalion took on drafts from two other regiments, the 50th and 51st Foot. This was a common practice at the time and it says much for the Royals' organisational capacity – the result of solid staff work by its officers – that the battalion was reinforced quickly and efficiently. As Dr Alan J. Guy put it in his account of 'The Army of the Georges' in *The Oxford Illustrated History of the British Army*, 'regimental history as we know it was created by a small number of long-suffering officers, rather than by the human traffic directed so quickly and so ruthlessly through the ranks'. In the spring of 1757 the Royals set sail from Cobh (or Queenstown) near Cork in a convoy of 50 transports guarded by 15 warships, which finally reached port at Halifax, Nova Scotia, at the beginning of July. Their landfall was followed by a period of intensive training for the fighting which lay ahead.

The British had been in North America since the beginning of the previous century, and during that time large numbers of settlers had poured into the eastern seaboard between Nova Scotia to the north and Georgia to the south. Originally these colonies were chartered bodies and the links with the Crown were operated with a light hand, but following the Restoration of King Charles II in 1660 the Crown exerted its influence and successive administrations brought the American colonies under tighter control. Naturally, this interference caused friction with the local elected colonial assemblies, many of whose members were instinctively suspicious of the Crown. Some were descended from families which had gone into exile in America during the civil wars or were Scots or Irishmen opposed to the Hanoverian succession. Another factor was the rivalry with France and the need to protect the colonies and to safeguard trade between them and the homeland. At the same time, the first half of the new century saw a period of expansion in the colonies as settlers began making their way westward over the Allegheny Mountains and the virgin territory which lay beyond. The undertaking was doubly dangerous because they would come into contact with the French, aided by their native American allies, who were attempting to link their holdings in Louisiana with their possessions to the north in present-day Canada. At the time there were only 50,000 French settlers in America, but although small in number they were well organised and well led, and proved a difficult enemy to beat.

In an attempt to bolster their American holdings the British sent fresh forces under General Edward Braddock in 1755, but they came under immediate and severe pressure from the French, who were attempting to push into the British colonies by advancing down the Hudson valley from their holdings in Canada on the far side of the St Lawrence River. The arrival of the new force in Nova Scotia (including the Royals) permitted the opening of a new front and the opportunity to strike a fresh blow against French interests. Their target was the huge fortress at Louisburg, which had been constructed by the French in 1720 as their main base on the continent to guard the approaches to the St Lawrence, provide a base for the French fleet and to protect the French fisheries. Constructed at huge expense, it was a symbol of French authority, but it had an Achilles heel: as the French had not developed farming on the island, they depended on British settlers for their supplies, and in 1745 Louisburg had fallen to local forces, backed by a British naval squadron. This was a crushing blow for the French, but the fortress was soon back in their hands. At the conclusion of the War of the Austrian Succession, Louisburg was returned to France in exchange for Madras under the terms of the Treaty of Aix-la-Chapelle, in 1748.

For the British, Louisburg was therefore a strategic target worth winning back, but it took a year before their combined naval and military forces were in position to begin the assault at the end of June 1758. Just under 200 ships took part in the operation, carrying 13,000 soldiers to a difficult landing on the east coast of Cape Breton Island. The two senior commanders, Admiral Edward Boscawen and General Lord Jeffrey Amherst, made heavy weather of the attack but the situation was retrieved by a young officer called James Wolfe, who had fought under Cumberland at Culloden in the rank of brevet-major. By moving artillery onto higher ground Wolfe was able to bombard the fort, which eventually surrendered in the third week of July. During the attack the Royals lost 2 officers and 13 men and just over 100 years later Louisburg was awarded to the regiment as its first American battle honour, the second being Niagara (1812–13). The capture of Louisburg inspired wild celebrations – bonfires were lit in Boston and Philadelphia, while 60,000 gallons of rum were drunk in Halifax, Nova Scotia – but its fall allowed the British to turn their attention to dealing with the vital corridor in the Hudson valley as the first step to ousting the French from Canada. The operations took place in 1759 – the famous 'year of victories', which saw French forces being defeated across the globe – but it proved to be a long-drawn-out and grinding process. While Wolfe, now a major-general, took a combined naval and military force up the St Lawrence to attack Quebec, subsidiary assaults were made up the valleys of the Hudson and the Ohio in Pennsylvania.

The Royals took part in the Hudson expedition and soon found themselves having to grapple with the arduous local topography. Not only did they have to move through the thick woodlands, but they had to learn to use small boats to deal with the obstacles provided by the River Hudson and Lake George. All the while, like the rest of the force, they were dressed in the same unyielding red uniforms which they had worn in Europe, complete with ruffles, gaiters and pipe-clayed belts. The ensemble might have looked smart, but it was hardly suitable for local conditions, and one sergeant remembered that he and his men were 'so tight and braced so firm that we almost stood like automata of wood'. On top of that they had to carry their muskets and ammunition knowing that in wet weather they were useless. In action, a soldier of The Royal Scots had to pull the cartridge from his pouch, remove the top by biting, shake powder into the priming pan, put the ball and the wadding into the barrel, press them home with the ramrod, return the ramrod to its position on the musket, fix the plug bayonet and then fire the weapon, which was only accurate over 50 paces. As battlefield tactics depended on the men following the firing procedure like clockwork it is no wonder that the best regiments insisted on strict discipline.

By mid-summer the French began retreating and the strategically important fort at Ticonderoga was in British hands, with Fort Crown Point to the north following later in the summer. To complete the victory Quebec fell to the British in September, although Wolfe was killed in the process, and by the end of 1759 French Canada was in British hands. At the end of the campaigning season the Royals moved south to winter quarters in New Jersey. The 2nd battalion's next contribution to the operations in North America was in some respects a reprise of their activities in the Highlands following the Jacobites' defeat at Culloden. During the conflict many of the native American peoples had generally sided with the French; although there had been discussions about entering into alliances with them, Amherst was not impressed by their qualities. 'They are a pack of lazy, rum-drinking people and little good, but if ever they are of use it will be when we can act offensively,' he told the Prime Minister, William Pitt. 'The French are much more afraid of them than they need be; numbers will increase their Terror and may have a good effect.' Some of their number were friendly, most notably the Iroquois people who lived along the Great Lakes and were suspicious of French expansionism, but others used the opportunity to attack the British forces. Even after the British and the colonists had gained the upper hand, hostile native Americans continued their attacks on British personnel and in one horrific incident a missing soldier was eventually found in the woods, 'killed and scalped; one of his arms was cut off; his bowels were taken out and cut into shreds, almost innumerable, with a long skewer thrust through his upper lip, nostrils and the crown of his head; the bloodhounds carried away his heart'.

Depredations of that kind were bound to attract revenge, and in the spring of 1760 the Royals contributed to a force of 400 soldiers sent south to Charleston in South Carolina to punish the Cherokee people, who had been attacking local settlers. According to the regiment's historian, Colonel Paterson, 'their instructions were to kill all the males they could and to burn their settlements'. This was punitive warfare with a vengeance and the force, under the command of Major Frederick Hamilton of the Royals, carried out its task with grim efficiency. Villages were put to the torch and Cherokee men were rounded up and slaughtered. Any resistance was crushed and not even the Cherokees' bloodthirsty taunts and battle cries – which, according to one historian, the Royals found 'more terrible than the slogan of the Gaels' – prevented the force from carrying out its grisly business.

In the modern world operations of this kind would be counted as atrocities, but from the very outset the relationship between the colonists and the native Americans had been fraught with tension and misunderstanding, which led to frequent uncontrolled outbreaks of violence on both sides. In some places, and during some periods, a live-and-let-live policy prevailed, but as the colonists began expanding their territories there were too many cases of each side cheating the other, with the result that the violence was often endemic. In the Royals' case the native Americans proved to be particularly resilient. It took a total of three operations before the Cherokees of South Carolina were finally crushed by the regiment's superior fire-power. The Royals' losses were 39 officers and men killed, plus a small number wounded.

During the same period the rest of the 2nd battalion was involved in the mopping-up operations along the St Lawrence before marching to New York in April 1761 prior to a new deployment in the West Indies. Their destination was the island of Dominica in the Windward group, a French possession, which was seized together with the island of St Vincent as part of Pitt's policy of wrapping up the West Indies. While this was happening, the rest of the 2nd battalion exchanged war against the Cherokees for a new engagement with Spanish forces on the island of Cuba. Britain's crushing defeat of France had thoroughly alarmed Spain, which felt that its own colonial holdings were being threatened, and hostilities between the two countries broke out early in 1762 when Spain declared war. Britain's first response was to invade Cuba by laying siege to the capital and main port, Havana. Following the seizure of Fort Moro, which was the key to the harbour entrance, Havana fell in the middle of July and the island was in British hands. More to the point, one third of Spain's naval strength was destroyed in the process. The Royals' losses were modest, but once again disease took a heavy toll on the 12,000-strong British forces, which had suffered 20 per cent casualties by the time they were withdrawn from the island in the following year. The conclusion of hostilities with France and Spain allowed a new peace treaty to be signed in Paris in 1763, and as a result Britain consolidated and added to its possessions in North America – Canada, Nova Scotia and Cape Breton were secured, together with Florida and the left bank of the Mississippi River while in the Caribbean area Britain received the islands of Grenada, St Vincent, Dominica and Tobago. Together with other important territorial gains in Africa, India and Europe these accessions confirmed Britain's position as a global power, but the same treaty also gave territorial advantages to France and Spain (one of them being the return of Cuba), which made further hostilities inevitable.

By then George III was on the throne. He was the first of the Hanoverian kings to be English born and bred but as Winston Churchill pointed out in the third volume of his *History of the English Speaking Peoples*, 'by the time George [III] died America had separated herself from the United Kingdom, the first British Empire had collapsed, and the King himself had gone mad'. The principal reason for that dire sequence of events was the great quarrel with the colonists in North America, which resulted in a disastrous war and defeat for the British Army. As we have seen, from the very beginning of the relationship there had been tensions between the Crown and the colonists, and these were exacerbated by the rapid expansion of British holdings after the conclusion of the Seven Years War. Another factor was the cost of waging the war. Fighting the French might have brought territorial additions, but the outlay had been borne entirely by the Treasury, and those costs included the expense of providing the armed forces that protected the American colonies. As the people of the colonies had benefited as a result, the British government believed that their cousins on the other side of the Atlantic should contribute to the overheads involved in fighting a generally successful war.

The trouble was that the government's fiscal policy was heavy-handed and maladroit, and as a result it caused a good deal of offence in the American colonies. A tax on molasses was followed by the equally unpopular Stamp Act in 1765. Both measures were unpopular and encouraged a good deal of unrest amongst the more radical elements, who had already voiced their concerns about the imposition of taxation by the London government. Eventually the cry 'no taxation without representation' became increasingly shrill in the colonies, and from 1770 skirmishes were increasingly breaking out, building up to the American War of Independence. The fighting only ended with the British surrender of Yorktown 11 years later. Fortunately, the Royals were not involved in that disastrous conflict.

Following service in North America and the West Indies, both battalions returned to Scotland and Ireland in the mid-1760s before receiving orders for further overseas deployments. In 1768 the 1st battalion sailed from Cork for a period of service in Gibraltar which lasted until 1775, while the 2nd battalion spent much of the same period in postings in England and Minorca, the island having come into British possession by the Treaty of Paris. Six years later, the 1st battalion was back in the West Indies to take part in an operation to protect British possessions in the Leeward Islands, but it ended in disaster when the garrison was obliged to surrender to superior French forces in February 1782. The following year hostilities were suspended amidst a general clamour for peace. France had quickly recognised the United States of America when it came into being in 1776 and, along with Spain, had used the War of Independence as a means of gaining revenge against Britain. However, as had happened so often earlier in the century, the peace treaties were only a postponement of the rivalry between the two countries. By 1793 the two countries were once again at loggerheads and were destined to be at war for the next 20 years.

The trigger was the revolution which swept through France in 1789 and destroyed for ever the power of the ruling royal family. In the early days, the events in France were welcomed outside that country as a necessary and much-needed change – 'bliss was it in that dawn to be alive' wrote the poet William Wordsworth – but the excesses of the 'Terror' quickly brought widespread disillusionment. In 1792 political prisoners began to be executed, and at the beginning of the following year King Louis XVI and his family were sent to the guillotine. At the same time, the revolution began to spread: France found itself at war with its traditional enemies Austria and Prussia, and in 1793 declared war against Britain. Facing up to the threat in a speech to parliament, Pitt said that the country was about to become involved in 'a war of honour, a war necessary to assert the spirit of the nation, and the dignity of the British name'. Alas, for all those fine words, Britain was once again ill-prepared to fight a major war. In the years following the defeat in North America, defence expenditure had been cut and the army had become something of a backwater. In a damning indictment of the state of the army at the end of the eighteenth century, one contemporary officer described an organisation that was without structure and lacking in aims and ambition: 'Each colonel of a regiment managed it according to his own notions, or neglected it altogether. There was no uniformity of drill or movement. Professional pride was rare; professional knowledge still more so.'

The Royals were not immune from the problems afflicting the rest of the army, but thanks to firm leadership the regiment emerged with a good deal of credit from its operational deployments in the first period of the war against revolutionary France. Some idea of its difficulties can be seen from the regiment's roll: when the 1st battalion was dispatched to Jamaica in 1790 its strength stood at under 500, but even then its troubles were not over. Ten years later the battalion received reinforcements in the shape of convicts who had joined the army rather than face deportation or the death sentence. Many of them were Irishmen who had taken part in the United Irishmen's uprising against British rule in 1798. For the first time, too, the make-up of the regiment's manpower was not predominantly Scottish, the bulk of the rank and file being English or Irish and, as happened throughout the army at that time, there were also soldiers from countries opposed to the aims of revolutionary France. In 1813 army returns showed that some 20 per cent of the total manpower of 250,000 soldiers was composed of French Royalists, soldiers from the German states and an assortment of Greeks, Corsicans, Africans and Caribbeans. This was a six-fold increase in the size of the army since 1793, when its total strength was little more than 40,000 and the percentage of foreigners indicates the extent of the recruiting problem and Britain's limited manpower resources.

Apart from a brief return to England between 1797 and 1800, the battalion served in the West Indies and Canada until 1815. The first aim of their deployment was to capture French possessions and territories which might have supported the French war effort, but the costs in manpower were horrific. In ten years some 80,000 soldiers served in the West Indies and half that number succumbed to illness, mainly yellow fever, leaving Major-General John Strawson, a recent historian of the period, to complain that 'no remote sugar island was worth such a price when the key to success against France lay not in the West Indies but on the continent of Europe'. Despite these difficulties, the Royals served with distinction in both of their main operational areas on the other side of the Atlantic. After taking possession of the islands of St Martin, St Thomas, St John and Santa Cruz – Danish possessions which the British deemed to be in breach of their owner's neutrality – a force including the Royals was sent to take possession of the Dutch holdings around the Demerara River in the present-day state of Guyana. Apart from the rigours of the climate and the monotonous diet it was a pleasant enough posting, and for the Royals there was the added distinction that their commanding officer, Lieutenant-Colonel Nicholson, also acted as governor of the territories. When they finally left in 1812, the battalion was commended for its 'correct discipline and military order' and, just as important as the commendations, it was once again up to strength, with over 1,200 officers and men. This time its destination was Canada, the deployment being ordered as a result of the American declaration of war on Britain on 18 June 1812, and the subsequent announcement that its war aims included invasion of its northern neighbour.

As was the case when Britain fought France for the possession of Canada, the key was the St Lawrence River and Quebec, but lacking a sizeable navy the US had to rely on its land forces which depended on large numbers of indifferently trained volunteers. Britain was also overstretched. It could rely only on some 10,000 British and Canadian troops and, with the war in Europe still raging, it was difficult to send reinforcements across the Atlantic. Fortunately, the joint British and Canadian forces had an able commander in General Isaac Brock and, in December 1813, a combined force, including the Royals, took possession of Fort Niagara. The campaign was marked by savage behaviour on both sides and quarter was rarely given, not least when native Americans were involved. During the advance into the United States in the summer of 1814 the Royals lost over 200 casualties killed or wounded at Chippawa and around the same number killed, wounded or taken prisoner at the drawn battle of Lundy's

Lane. The end of the fighting in Europe brought this 'futile and unnecessary conflict' to an end, the main result being the fixing of the border between the US and Canada and the emergence of the US as an independent power. In the summer of 1815, the 1st battalion returned to Britain and spent the rest of the year garrisoned in Edinburgh before returning to Ireland.

Being stationed in Edinburgh was a bonus in that it gave the men access to the city at a time when it was expanding its horizons – the Georgian new town had been built towards the end of the previous century – but the garrison provisions in the castle were a mixed blessing. In its favour, Edinburgh was one of the few cities in Britain that could offer accommodation for a complete infantry regiment, but conditions inside the castle were not of the best. The barracks lacked proper washing facilities and basic sanitation, and in winter there were few incentives to encourage men to maintain basic hygiene. Sleeping space was cramped, with each man being allotted 450 cubic feet, and beds were not provided, the alternative being straw-filled palliasses whose contents were changed every two months. Men slept together, cooked together, ate together, washed together and cleaned their kit and weapons together. According to an infantry officer of the period – not a Royal Scot, but his views are typical – it was a noisome world which required tolerance and a strong stomach:

> In winter the men would block up all the ventilation with old sacking, etc . . . and when I had to visit the rooms in the morning as Duty Officer, the atmosphere was so nauseating that I felt disinclined to touch my breakfast afterwards. Of course, the soldiers had only an outside tap to wash from, which was often froze up, and even when it was not, you may imagine that few of them were bold enough to strip and swill themselves in the cold and

darkness of a January morning . . . You can smell some
soldiers' feet before you enter their rooms.

The fortunes of the 2nd battalion were somewhat different, and
their experiences at the end of the eighteenth century provide
a more conventional picture of this phase of the war against
France. Although they did not know it at the time, the Royals' first
encounter with the French would involve them with the man whose
personality and leadership qualities would influence the direction
of the war: Napoleon Bonaparte, a young Corsican artillery officer,
and later the Emperor of France. The engagement took place
at Toulon in the summer of 1793, after the town and its naval
port had declared their loyalty to King Louis XVII. Marseilles
and Lyons followed suit but the revolts were quickly put down,
leaving Toulon in Royalist hands but desperate for reinforcement
from the powers opposed to France. Britain's response was to
send in Admiral Alexander Hood's Mediterranean fleet, but his
22 warships could not hold the heavily fortified port unaided and
he made an immediate appeal for the dispatch of 50,000 troops
to mount the shore defences. Desperate attempts were made to
find the necessary forces, but with the British Army's manpower
resources in a parlous state, and its available troops deployed in
the West Indies and Flanders (under the Duke of York), it was
an impossible task. The Gibraltar garrison, including 2nd Royal
Scots, was shipped in and, together with a mixed force of French
Royalists, Neapolitans, Piedmontese and Spaniards, they formed
the allied army for the defence of Toulon.

For a time it seemed as if the defenders might have been able to
secure the port. The French had to deal with the threat of Austrian
invasion and the presence of the British expeditionary force in
Flanders, but the Committee of Public Safety, France's ruling
body, dealt with each threat in turn before switching its attention

to Toulon. Force of numbers decided the issue – the defending garrison numbered 12,000, the French besiegers three times that number – but the attack was also helped by Napoleon Bonaparte's astute handling of the artillery at Fort l'Aiguillette which guarded the entrance to the harbour. The Royals played their full part in the defence of the perimeter, but on 17 December the defences broke and the defenders had to withdraw to the safety of Hood's fleet. Desperate attempts were made to scuttle the French fleet and blow up the port installations, and while these were only partially successful, Hood's warships were at least able to withdraw safely. With them they took the 2nd battalion which was next sent to Elba prior to an attack on Corsica by a small force under the command of Lieutenant-Colonel John Moore, an enterprising officer from Glasgow who was destined to make his name, and lose his life, in the fighting against Napoleon in Spain and Portugal. In the first action against French defences at Martello Bay, on 17 February 1794, Moore commanded the attacking columns, which included the flank companies of the Royals, consisting of grenadiers and light infantry. This successful action was a prelude to the capture of most of the island, and Moore's diary records that the Royals played a prominent part in capturing the last obstacle, the port of Calvi. On 19 July the battalion's grenadiers, under the command of Captain McDonald 'advanced with their bayonets, with such intrepidity, that the French gave way, and ran out of the fort'. After acting as garrison troops, the battalion was sent to Elba to carry out a similar policing role before returning to Gibraltar in 1797.

The battalion's next operational deployment took it to the Netherlands as part of a force including Russian infantry, which was aimed at encouraging the House of Orange to throw in its lot with the allies. Although the allies had naval superiority, there was little coordination of the ground forces. A successful attack was made on the French positions at Egmont-op-Zee on 2 October which forced the enemy to retire, but a fortnight later so little progress had been made that the forces were withdrawn to England. One of the reasons for the French army's ability to halt the allied advance had been its use of *tirailleurs*, skirmishing sharpshooters whose accuracy of fire and speed of movement caused high casualties amongst the advancing British redcoats. Similar troops, known as *Jäger*, had served in the Austrian and Prussian armies earlier in the century and had fought under British command in America, and the usefulness of these light troops encouraged the British Army to found a Corps of Riflemen in 1800. A number of officers and men from the 2nd battalion were transferred to the new regiment, which later fought as The Rifle Brigade (95th Regiment), and was made distinctive by innovations such as rifle-green uniforms with black buttons, bugle commands and a rapid marching pace.

If the Royals' participation in the war to date could not be counted as an overall success, the same could not be said about their next deployment as part of General Sir Ralph Abercromby's expedition to engage Napoleon's army of the East in Egypt in 1801. This was designed to oust French forces from Egypt and to relieve the threat they posed to Britain's holdings in India, but the operation was a hazardous one. Not only were the French already in position at Alexandria, but they had more artillery and possessed cavalry. They were also in a position to oppose the amphibious landings but, thanks to strict training in advance of the landings, the British forces came safely ashore at Aboukir Bay and were able to repel the main French attack on 21 March. Under Moore's operational direction – he was by then a major-general – the defending British forces showed great coolness under fire, and a month later Alexandria was in their hands. To recognise their courage, all the regiments involved in the expedition were

FOUR

CHANGE AND DECAY: FROM WATERLOO TO THE CRIMEA

The Treaty of Amiens not only failed to produce a lasting peace, it was also unsuccessful in discouraging Napoleon from pursuing his territorial ambitions; as such it fully deserved the description visited on it by contemporaries who condemned it as 'a peace which all men are glad of, but no man can be proud of'. Worse, the end of hostilities persuaded the British government to reduce the size of its armed forces: plans were put in place to halve the number of warships and to set the strength of the army at 95,000 soldiers (plus 18,000 for the Irish garrison). Heightened tensions with France eventually postponed the economies, but the fact that Britain was considering defence cutbacks clearly convinced Napoleon to take a bolder line in his foreign policy. The spark came from a disputed claim over possession of the island of Malta, which had been captured by Britain in 1800, giving it control of the Mediterranean. However, with most of Europe cowed, Napoleon's ultimate aim was to invade Britain with an army 200,000-strong and led by his most experienced field commanders, including the future marshals Bernadotte, Soult and Ney. It was a moment of great danger, but in October 1805 the enterprise was foiled by Admiral Lord Nelson's famous victory at Trafalgar and the destruction of the French and Spanish fleet. The repercussions were enormous: Napoleon had to give up all hope of invading his most powerful enemy, the Royal Navy had won command of the sea and Britain was given a fresh opportunity to pursue the war against France on the continent of Europe. Before that latter stage could be reached, though, the country had to build up an army capable of taking on and defeating France's seemingly impregnable land forces. To do that, the problem of recruitment had to be addressed, funds had to be made available to purchase equipment and the budget had to be increased to allow higher rates of pay. Finally, a stop had to be made to the policy of attacking faraway French colonial possessions which brought cheap victories but accomplished nothing in defeating the enemy.

At that crucial stage, the army was helped by the emergence of two soldiers who would be critical to its development in the next ten years of the war against Napoleonic France. The first was John Moore who had had the Royals under his command in Corsica and who had emerged as a superb field commander after his magnificent victory at Aboukir Bay. Aged 40 in 1802, he was very much a soldier's soldier, who believed in the value of training and always put the needs of his soldiers first. In common with other great leaders, he argued that all ranks should share the privations and dangers of service in the field, and he was insistent that soldiers in authority should not order their men to do anything unless they were also prepared to carry out the same duty. Above all, he was committed to the regimental system, seeing unit cohesion as the best means of maintaining morale and instilling discipline. 'It is evident that not only the officers but that each individual soldier knows what he has to do,' he remarked after inspecting his old regiment, the 52nd Foot (Oxfordshire Light Infantry). 'Discipline is carried on without severity, the officers are attached to the men and the men to the officers.' Knighted and promoted lieutenant-general, he was responsible for organising Britain's home defences and in 1808, following an aborted plan to invade Sweden, he was put in command of the forces in the north of Spain, his orders being 'to co-operate with the Spanish armies in the expulsion of the French from that kingdom'.

The other soldier to influence the development of the British Army during that period was quite different. Arthur Wellesley, later the Duke of Wellington, had come to the fore fighting in India in the wars against the Marathas – he counted Assaye, 1803, as his greatest victory – and in the Peninsula he was to emerge as a skilful manager of men and a master tactician who had the successful commander's ability to read ground and keep one step ahead of the enemy. Unlike Moore, he kept his men at a distance and was a rigid disciplinarian who was perhaps more respected than admired by his soldiers. Known throughout his army as 'Old Nosey' he was never popular and is best remembered for his infamous comment that the soldiers under his command were 'the scum of the earth' who enlisted only for the chance to get drunk and who could be kept in control only by the threat of the lash and the gallows. There was, of course, more to Wellesley than hauteur, and no leader could have got so much out of his men if he had treated them only with contempt. While he deplored his soldiers' depraved habits – it was true that on active service drink and violence were part and parcel of their off-duty lives – Wellesley also recognised that these same men were capable of being turned into a loyal and disciplined army:

> People talk of enlisting for their fine military feeling – all
> stuff – no such thing. Some of our men enlist for having

got bastard children – some for minor offences – many more for drink; but you can hardly conceive such a set brought together, and it really is wonderful that we should have made them the fine fellows they are.

Somewhere between Moore and Wellesley the red-coated soldier of the first decade of the nineteenth century comes into focus. Amongst them were the men of The Royal Scots. As part of the expansion of the army in 1804, following the realisation that the French were serious in their threat to mount an invasion, the Royals increased in size to meet the need for more infantry. On 1 December 1804, a 3rd battalion was raised at Hamilton in Lanarkshire but, due to recruiting problems across the country, it did not reach full strength until the summer of 1808, having spent time in stations in Scotland, England and Ireland. At the same time a 4th battalion was also raised, but it was used principally for recruiting purposes and for providing drafts for the regiment's three other battalions. It did not see any service until August 1813, when it formed part of a force sent to Stralsund to encourage the Swedes to join the allies, and in the following year it was engaged in operations against French forces in the Netherlands, where it found itself in the unfortunate position of being forced to surrender its colours to the enemy. The battalion's bad luck continued in the summer of 1814 when it was sent to Canada, only to be involved in a shipwreck in which the battalion lost all its kit. On its return to Europe as an occupation force, following the final defeat of Napoleon, it was disbanded at the beginning of 1816.

What kind of life did an infantry soldier in The Royal Scots experience in the war against Napoleon? In some respects little had changed since Marlborough's day. Regiments still consisted of ten companies, with eight in the centre and two slightly larger flank companies composed of grenadiers and light infantrymen. Wherever possible the latter formations comprised more experienced soldiers, with older veterans and newcomers in the centre. The standard weapon was still the smooth-bore flintlock rifle, whose effective range was around 100 yards, which meant that infantry formations had to get close to the opposition before opening fire in disciplined volleys. By far the biggest change in tactics was the introduction of light infantrymen and the use of more accurate weapons, such as the Baker rifle, which allowed its users to be known as 'sharp-shooters'. As used by the French, and later by the British, these new elite troops acted as skirmishers and, acting independently ahead of the main forces, they brought greater flexibility to the battlefield by opening up gaps and paving the way for the deployment of heavy infantry and cavalry to exploit the initial breakthrough.

In return, conditions for the rank and file improved – but only gradually. By the end of the 1790s a private infantry soldier was paid a shilling a day, with half that amount being deducted for stoppages such as rations and laundry, and on signing up a bounty of 12 guineas was payable. In place of signing on for life 'limited service' was also instituted to allow soldiers to serve three different periods of seven years, with discharge on half-pay in between. Marriage was permitted, but most regiments did not encourage their soldiers to take wives, owing to the difficulties of housing them. On home service most regiments turned a blind eye to the number of women 'on the strength' – that is, those entitled to quarter and rations – but on active service it was a different matter. An army order limited the number of wives to six per hundred soldiers and those selected (by ballot) were supposed to help as unofficial nurses and cooks, putting up with the same hardships endured by their husbands and the rest of the battalion. If their husbands died or were killed, the usual practice was for the woman to marry another soldier in the regiment, usually within a day or so of being widowed. It was not a relationship for the squeamish, and the army's official view was summed up by the editor of the *United Service Journal* at the beginning of the nineteenth century: 'the admission of females is an indulgence, contingent on their own conduct and usefulness and the due accommodation and recreations of the men'. In other words, if the wives wanted to be accepted by the regiment, they had to make themselves useful.

The appearance of the soldiers in the Royals also changed during the Wellington years. Breeches gave way to grey trousers, which meant an end to gaiters with their awkward buttons, shorter red coats replaced the traditional tailed coat, and a new stove-pipe hat was introduced to offer greater protection to the wearer. Soldiers received two pairs of shoes, but each shoe was the same size and shape, a practice which continued until 1847. Less importance was placed on the management of hair, which was worn shorter, and the unloved stock – a piece of stiff leather which supported the high collar – gradually disappeared. At this stage in their development there was nothing to distinguish the Royals from the other line infantry regiments of the British Army. Slowly, their soldiers were gaining a more uniform appearance to match their growing professionalism in the field.

At the end of 1805, the 2nd battalion transferred the bulk of its officers and men to the River Demerara to reinforce the 1st battalion, while a cadre of 72 officers and men, many of them sick and enfeebled, returned to Britain to regroup with reinforcements from the newly formed 3rd and 4th battalions as well as from other line regiments including the 26th (Cameronians) Foot. Once up to an operational strength of just over 1,000 soldiers in April 1807, the 2nd battalion set sail for the first time for India. After an eventful voyage – one of the transports was afflicted by scurvy, another was attacked while taking on water – they formed part of the British garrison in British India, a country which the military historian Correlli Barnett has described as 'the greatest formative influence on the life, language and legend of the British army . . . India, with its heat, stinks and noise, its enveloping dust, became the British Army's second home – perhaps its first'. For the Royals, the 2nd battalion's posting was to be the first of many similar deployments for the regiment in the Indian sub-continent.

With the 1st and 2nd battalions deployed overseas, and with the 4th battalion based at home as a depot formation until the final years of the war, the task of engaging Napoleon's armies fell to the 3rd Royal Scots, who were destined to take part in the major campaigns to defeat them in the Peninsula and at Waterloo. However, at the time of the opening of the front in Spain and Portugal it did not seem possible that Britain's smaller army would be capable of engaging and defeating Napoleon's *Grande Armée*. The past few years had seen the defeat of Prussia, Austria and Russia – the last had encouraged the Emperor Alexander to enter a compact with Napoleon to crush Britain – and by the summer of 1807 it seemed that all of Europe lay at France's feet. To complete the domination, Napoleon turned his attention to Spain and Portugal. The first was subjugated by the simple ruse of enticing the Spanish King Charles IV to Bayonne and forcing him to abdicate, imposing military rule in the country under Charles's brother, Joseph. The second, England's oldest ally, was then invaded from Spain by an army commanded by Marshal Junot. Both were daring, if ruthless, plans and both were foiled by the refusal of the people of Spain and Portugal to accept French domination, and by the British decision to send forces to assist them in resisting the invasion.

The first part of the campaign ended in farce. Following Wellesley's stunning victory at Vimiero on 21 August 1808, the French army was allowed to retreat back to France in ships provided by the Royal Navy. The agreement sickened Wellesley, who remarked that his officers could 'go and shoot red-legged partridges' – and it allowed Napoleon to assume command of military operations in the Peninsula. At the same time, a new army under Moore's direction marched from Lisbon into northern Spain through Salamanca towards Valladolid, his aim being to link up with friendly Spanish forces. Backing for the enterprise was provided by 17,000 additional troops under the command of Lieutenant-General Sir David Baird, a tough battle-hardened Scot whose forces landed in Corunna in October. Amongst them was the 3rd battalion, which took an early and important part in the campaign when one of the Royals' officers intercepted a French signal announcing the defeat of the Spanish army and Napoleon's subsequent move to intercept Moore's army. The information persuaded Moore to fall back on Corunna and the Royals took part in that heroic fighting retreat over the snow-covered winter mountains which left the men 'unwashed, unshorn and unspeakably filthy' on their return to Britain in January 1809. During the final phase of the fighting at Corunna Moore was killed, but at least the bulk of his army had escaped.

Following their participation in a brief amphibious raid on a French naval base at Walcheren in Flanders the Royals were back in Portugal in the spring of 1810 in a new force under Wellesley's command. For the next three years the British Army and its allies were to be involved in a war of movement and attrition as Wellesley engaged the enemy when it was prudent, and showed that he knew 'when to retreat and to dare to do so'. Throughout the campaign, Wellesley was uncomfortably aware that defeat would not only lead to disaster for Britain but would allow Napoleon to remove his troops for service elsewhere in Europe, where Austria had once again entered the fray. 'As this is the last army England has,' noted Wellesley, 'we must take care of it.' It was a sound policy, but it did not always entail keeping his men wrapped up in cotton wool. Fighting along the River Tagus Wellesley defeated the French at Talavera, for which he was ennobled as Viscount Wellington, and following victories at Busaco and the Lines of Torres Vedras, Portugal was liberated a year later. Ahead lay the bruising battles of Fuentes de Onoro, Ciudad Rodrigo, Badajoz, Vittoria and Salamanca, which forced the French to pull out of Spain. All were hard-fought battles and for the Royals none was so ferociously fought as the struggle at San Sebastian between 18 and 31 July 1813, when the 3rd battalion formed part of the 'forlorn hope', the soldiers who made the initial assault on the fortress. A contemporary account by an 'old soldier' gives a vivid account of the conditions which would have faced the Royals as they went into the attack:

> Slaughter, tumult and disorder continued; no command could be heard, the wounded struggling to free themselves from under the bleeding bodies of their dead comrades; the enemy's guns within a few yards at every fire opening a bloody lane amongst our people, who closed up and, with shouts of terror as the lava burned them up, pressed on to destruction – officers starting forward with an heroic impulse, carried on their men to yawning breach and glittering steel, which still belched out flames of scorching death.

By the time that San Sebastian fell, the Royals had lost 140 killed and 388 wounded, but the war in Spain was now over. Two months later, on 7 October, the 3rd battalion's light company had the distinction of being the first British troops to cross the frontier into France, where it took part in the final phase of the fighting in a force commanded by Lieutenant-General Sir John Hope, the investment of the French army at Bayonne. In the summer of

1814, following Napoleon's defeat and abdication, the battalion sailed for Ireland. Once again, as had happened so often when Britain was facing defeat in Europe, the British Army proved to be equal to the task and in the Peninsular War emerged as a tough and battle-hardened force, the equal of any in Europe. True, the campaigning was also marked by numerous examples of criminal behaviour, with soldiers running amok after victory, as happened with the Royals at San Sebastian, and order was often kept only by severe punishments such as the liberal use of the lash. But despite all the hardships regimental pride remained intact. By the end of the campaign, the 3rd battalion had more Irishmen and Englishmen than Scots in its ranks, but as an unknown soldier in Wellington's army remarked about the men who served with him, 'come what may, in brawls or battles, he would defend the honour of the Regiment. There never was a court martial charge of cowardice against a man in the ranks.'

The British soldier would need all that fortitude and more when Napoleon broke out of his exiled imprisonment on Elba on 26 February 1815 and set about reclaiming his position. Using the magic of his name, he rallied the veterans of his old armies and challenged the rest of Europe to respond. The result was the Waterloo campaign which led to his final defeat at the hands of the British and the Prussians, but as Wellington remarked after his final triumph over the French emperor, it had been a close-run thing. Britain and her allies had lost 16,000 casualties, the Prussians lost 7,000 and the French losses were computed at 25,000. Fought on 18 June 1815, the Battle of Waterloo put an end to Napoleon's ambitions – afterwards he was exiled on the Atlantic island of St Helena – and it is counted as one of the greatest battles ever fought by the British Army. The triumph is made more memorable by the fact that Wellington was outnumbered, his British troops had been depleted – 14,000

Peninsula veterans had been sent to America – and many of the allied German and Dutch soldiers were inexperienced. Against his enemies' advantages, Wellington enjoyed close cooperation with the Prussian commander, Field Marshal Blücher, and as a result allied intelligence about the French dispositions was more accurate. In the opening stages at Quatre Bras on 16/17 June the French failed to split the allied army, and the following day the allies survived a number of French hammer-blows, standing firm in the face of wave after wave of enemy attacks on their lines. During the Waterloo campaign, the 3rd Royal Scots served in Lieutenant-General Sir Thomas Picton's 5th Division, fighting in the centre at Quatre Bras where they won praise for their gallantry in holding their defensive square, together with the 28th (North Gloucestershire) Foot. The following day they bore the brunt of an attack by the French 2nd Corps, a feat that was all the more remarkable as they had been soaked to the skin by heavy rain the previous night. During the battle the battalion almost lost its King's Colour when Ensign Kennedy was killed while carrying it forward, but the dead officer and the colour were retrieved by a sergeant who braved enemy fire to bring both back to the Royals' lines. The 3rd battalion was disbanded in 1817.

Waterloo finally put a stop to the long years of warfare with France, and as a result Britain was able to reduce its defence spending. The size of the army was gradually decreased and the subsequent deterioration in conditions had a deleterious effect on recruiting, with fewer young men prepared to look on soldiering as a suitable career. For the Royals this meant that they had to depend on large numbers of Irishmen to keep up to strength. Regimental rolls show that while the majority of the officers were Scots, the rank and file were Irish, English or Scots with the last usually being in a minority. Even so, the Royals managed to maintain their links with

Scotland. Despite the fact that both battalions spent most of the first half of the nineteenth century stationed overseas, the regiment maintained a presence at home and at various times a battalion, or part of a battalion, was stationed in Edinburgh, Glasgow or another Scottish town. Defence cutbacks and stagnation also affected the regiment's appearance. Uniforms were often shabby and in constant need of repair, weapons were reported as being unserviceable and after one inspection in 1824 the 1st battalion's colours were found to be 'completely worn out' and had to be replaced. Service overseas also affected a regiment's ability to recruit. While there were always young men who jumped at the idea of serving in exotic places like India, largely because it had the advantage of offering lower expenses and an adventurous style of life, the pattern of long years abroad could be a disincentive to recruiting. In the period between 1815 and 1850, the Royals' two battalions served at one time or another in the West Indies, Canada, India and Gibraltar, which meant that some soldiers never served in home stations. This was not unusual: of the army's total of 112 infantry battalions in 1846, 87 were stationed abroad, in postings which could last up to 20 years. Deaths caused by warfare and disease meant that many recruits never returned to their homes and families. For the Royals, it helped that during this period the regiment had a number of distinguished colonels with sound military connections, including the Duke of Kent (1801–20), a field marshal whose daughter became Queen Victoria, and Lord Lynedoch (1838–43), a veteran of the Peninsular War who raised the 90th (Perthshire) Light Infantry in 1794. Later it became the 2nd battalion of The Cameronians, better known within the army as the 2nd Scottish Rifles.

As we have seen, the 2nd battalion had sailed to India in 1807 as part of the British garrison in the sub-continent and it remained there until 1831, when it returned to Scotland, then Ireland, before being deployed in the West Indies and Canada. This meant that from 1807 until 1846 the battalion spent only five years at a home station in Scotland or Ireland. By far the most interesting posting was the 24 years spent in India. For most of that period it was involved in internal security wars as Britain consolidated its presence in the sub-continent. The 2nd battalion took part in operations against local forces in Nagpore (1817) and Asseerghur (1819) and was one of the British regiments involved in the invasion of Burma in 1825, fighting in a joint British–Indian army under the command of General Archibald Campbell. Its first action saw it advancing up the River Irrawaddy by steamboat and it was present at the investment of the capital, Ava, which brought the war to a conclusion in 1826. As a result, Britain annexed the coastal area centred on Chittagong and the Burmese agreed to stop interfering in Assam, the reason for the war in the first place. The Burmese war brought home to the government the need to reinforce India and to improve the system of recruiting, but the lessons were learned at a cost. During the fighting the British lost 3,000 soldiers to disease, 427 being members of the 2nd battalion.

The Royals returned to India in the summer of 1826 and were stationed at Bangalore, a pleasant garrison town or cantonment in the state of Mysore, which gave them time to recuperate from the hardships of campaigning in Burma. From contemporary accounts it seems to have been an agreeable posting, at least for the officers, who enjoyed a round of 'monthly balls, private parties, amateur theatricals, mess dinners, riding, driving, horse racing etc'. For the rank and file conditions were somewhat different, but the differences in standing between the officers and the men of the Royals did not make India an unattractive posting. Due to the heat, the day began early and parades and inspections were finished by nine o'clock. Those soldiers with wives on the strength generally enjoyed better conditions than they would at

There was, though, more to the war than the oft-rehearsed catalogue of blunders redeemed by basic human courage and a refusal to surrender to overwhelming odds. For all the participants – Britain, France, Russia, the Ottoman Empire and, later, Sardinia – the war ended the long peace of 1815 and set in train the succession of small European conflicts and power struggles which dominated the second half of the nineteenth century. It began in the summer of 1853 as a petty squabble between the Orthodox and Catholic churches over the rights to the holy sites in Jerusalem – the actual spark was possession of the key to the main door of the Church of the Nativity in Bethlehem – and quickly spread to become a war to prevent Russian expansionist ambitions in the Black Sea geo-strategic region. Tsar Nicholas I entertained hopes of using a perceived weakness of Ottoman rule to gain influence in the Balkans, where there was a significant Slavic population, and began exerting diplomatic and military pressure on Constantinople. Matters escalated relentlessly and quickly brought the main participants to the verge of war. In the summer of 1853, Russian forces invaded the Ottoman principalities of Moldavia and Wallachia, a move which forced Turkey to declare war in October. From that point onwards a general conflict became inevitable as both Britain and France were opposed to the Russian moves and wished to shore up Ottoman rule. At the beginning of 1854 a Turkish naval squadron was overwhelmed and destroyed by the Russian fleet at Sinope and a few weeks later the British and French fleets sailed into the Black Sea, followed by the mobilisation of both countries' land forces. In reply to a question in the House of Lords on 14 February 1854, the Foreign Secretary, the Earl of Clarendon, admitted that 'we are drifting towards war'.

War was eventually declared at the beginning of April, and command of the British expeditionary force was given to Lord

Raglan who, as Lord Fitzroy Somerset, had been Wellington's military secretary in the Peninsula and who had an unblemished, if unspectacular, military career. His connection to Wellington counted for much, as did his personal courage (he lost his right arm at Waterloo) and his ability to get on with the French allies (he spoke fluent French, but discommoded his allies in the Crimea by referring to them as 'the enemy'). The 1st battalion was part of Raglan's force and left for 'the seat of war' (as it was called) on 3 March, bound first for Malta and then for Varna in present-day Bulgaria. The Royals formed part of the 3rd Division which was under the command of Lieutenant-General Sir Richard England, an experienced infantryman and veteran of the fighting against Napoleon. On the force's departure *The Times* called it 'the finest army that has ever left these shores'.

It soon became clear that the encomium was misplaced. No one doubted the courage of the soldiers who went to war with the cheers of their fellow countrymen ringing in their ears, but the direction of the war was soon revealed as a shambles. By the time the British and French forces arrived in the principalities the Russians had withdrawn, following an aggressive deployment by the Austrian army. By then cholera had set in and within weeks of landing the allies had lost 10,000 casualties. With public confidence in the enterprise waning, the decision was taken to attack and destroy the large Russian naval base at Sevastopol on the south-western side of the Crimean peninsula. For the allied armies this meant landing at Eupatoria to the north and attacking down the coastline towards Sevastopol, the idea being to gain the objective before winter set in. The first encounter took place on 20 September, when the allies attacked the Russians at the River Alma, and to begin with the portents were good. In a hard-pounding battle, the Russians were forced to retire and although it was not a decisive victory it encouraged hopes that the campaign would soon be over. During the battle the 3rd Division formed part of the reserve and as the British forces went into the attack an officer was heard to remark: 'Look at that, the Queen of England would give her eyes to see it.' The harsh reality was that the Alma, like the other Crimean battles, was marred by a lack of planning, faulty reconnaissance and an absence of command and control, its only plus-point being the courage and fortitude displayed by the soldiers taking part.

The Alma also turned out to be a missed opportunity as no immediate move was made on Sevastopol and the Russians were allowed to regroup. As a result, the allies were forced into a further battle at Balaclava on 25 October, which is remembered chiefly for the futile, though gallant, Charge of the Light Brigade, and the subsequent Battle of Inkerman 11 days later. Remembered as 'a soldier's battle' (which battle is not?), Inkerman was fought by the Russians to break the allies' siege lines outside Sevastopol, and it almost worked. The British were caught by surprise and the fighting quickly became a close-quarter struggle with ferocious hand-to-hand fighting which one survivor (Lieutenant-Colonel E.B. Hamley, Royal Artillery) remembered with awe some years later: 'Colonels of regiments led on small parties and fought like subalterns, captains like privates. Once engaged, every man was his own general.' The British lost 597 killed and 1,860 wounded; looking at the dead piled high at one gun emplacement, a French officer exclaimed, '*Quel abattoir!*' Astonishingly, given the ferocity of the fighting, the Royals only lost one soldier killed.

Their good fortune did not hold. Winter set in and on 10 November a huge storm left a trail of devastation in the British port at Balaclava, adding to the army's growing supply problems. As the weather worsened the conditions deteriorated, leaving an officer attached to the Light Division to bemoan the 'sad misery amongst the men'. During that long hard winter in which the shortcomings of the supply and medical systems were exposed the Royals lost over three hundred men to illness while only seven were killed in action. Amongst those who suffered were the wives who had accompanied the battalion and who were forced to share their husbands' privation, although as Sergeant Thomas Smith remembered they 'occupied themselves with washing clothes and darning socks and busied themselves in other ways to provide a semblance of comfort for the heroes who fought in the Alma heights or in the fog of Inkerman against such heavy odds'. So dreadful were the conditions that Captain Henry Clifford, an officer in the Rifle Brigade, wrote home at the beginning of 1855 admitting that of the 25,000 soldiers who began the siege of Sevastopol in the autumn, only 12,000 were still fit for duty. 'If the weather, with its consequent hardships, is to continue till the end of March,' he added, 'what will become of us?' By then the problems facing the army had become a matter of scandal at home, thanks largely to the exposures published by *The Times*, whose correspondent, William Howard Russell, was an assiduous reporter of the hardships endured by the soldiers.

The Royals were next in action in June in a series of attacks mounted by the British and French on the Russian defences which accomplished nothing but created further high casualties. In the first assault on a position known as the Quarries, the French lost 5,443 casualties, the British 671. By then the 2nd battalion had arrived in the Crimea and it took part in the next assault on the Great Redan, which began after a huge artillery assault on the night of 17 June. Unfortunately, it was a cloudless night and the element of surprise was lost when the Russians observed the British regiments moving into the forward trenches. During this action Private Joseph Prosser, 2nd battalion, prevented a soldier of another regiment from deserting to the enemy and, following another act of high courage in August, he was awarded the regiment's first Victoria Cross, the medal for gallantry which was instituted by Queen Victoria in January 1856. Both battalions were involved in the final attacks on Sevastopol in September when the siege finally came to an end after the Russians surrendered their seemingly impregnable position. Ahead lay another winter in the field and it was not until the following spring that peace talks brought the war to an end, but most of the long-suffering regiments, including the Royals, were not sent home until June 1856. The 1st battalion returned to Ireland while the 2nd battalion was sent to Gibraltar after a short stay in Malta.

FIVE

HIGH NOON: FROM THE CRIMEA TO THE BOER WAR

Once the war was over and the Crimea had been evacuated, the War Office started counting the cost, not just in financial outlay but also in human terms. Efforts were made to learn from the experience, although these were often aimless and the sweeping reforms which might have been expected failed to materialise. The exception covered the sanitary conditions facing the soldiers in the field and at the huge military hospital at Scutari. Since most of the casualties were due to illness and disease – only 1 in 10 of the total British casualty list of 19,584 had died in action in the Crimea – the results of two commissions into sanitary and nursing conditions did produce some change. In February 1855, the first Hospital Commission produced important reforms and a second Sanitary Commission produced quick results at Balaclava, where a strict regime for the troops' hygiene lowered the death rate. Only in the field of the army's administration in the Crimea was there vacillation and the commission investigating the Commissariat (supply) Department exonerated the army and placed the blame for deficiencies on pre-war Treasury restrictions.

The terrible conditions endured by the army also encouraged a flurry of interest in soldiers' welfare. In 1857, a Royal Sanitary Commission investigated the conditions in barracks and military hospitals and its findings merely underlined the nation's low opinion of its armed forces. The mortality rate amongst soldiers was double that of the civilian population, with the home-based army losing 20.8 per cent of its strength due to illness or disease. The Commissioners placed the blame on unsanitary conditions, poor diet and the 'enervating mental and bodily effects produced by ennui'. Their recommendations led to a steady improvement in the soldier's lot: a programme was instituted to improve ventilation, sanitary conditions and waste disposal in British barracks and steps were taken to provide soldiers with better leisure facilities in an attempt to cut down on the scourge of drunkenness. Two years later parliament voted £726,841 for the improvements but the reforms proved to be a slow and expensive process and it was not until 1861 that the Commission on Barracks and Hospitals could report that 45 barracks had proper lavatories in place of the cesspits that had been there for generations.

Changes were also made to the operation and structure of the army but, given the prevailing conservatism, many of the proposed reforms took time to take root. A Staff College came into being at Camberley to provide further intensive training for promising officers, the Crimean conflict having exposed the weakness of reliance on regimental soldiering alone. Recruitment problems were addressed by introducing short-service enlistment, the number of years being reduced from twenty-one years to six years with the Colours and six in the Reserves. As for the purchase of officers' commissions, which had been much criticised during the war, it was not abolished until 1871, the magazine *Punch* observing in a 'Notice to Gallant but Stupid Young Gentlemen' that they could only purchase their commissions 'up to the 31st day of October. After that you will be driven to the cruel necessity of deserving them.' As it turned out, the reform had little effect in regiments like The Royal Scots, where the low rates of pay and the high cost of living meant that officers continued to come from the same social background as before – mostly from the upper and professional classes and the landed gentry. On the equipment side, the first breech-loading rifles were introduced in 1868 (the Snider followed by the Martini-Henry and the Enfield), but the army's traditional red coats were not replaced by khaki until the 1880s, when campaigning in the deserts of Egypt and Sudan made ceremonial dress inappropriate for operation service. (The change to khaki was gradual and was not made official until 1902.) In appearance, the Royals in the Crimea looked remarkably similar to their forebears in the Peninsula nearly 50 years earlier.

For the next 60 years, Britain was to play no part in the wars which were fought in Europe, the main conflict being the Franco–Prussian War of 1871. Instead, the army was to spend most of its time engaged in colonial policing duties in various parts of Britain's imperial holdings. For the 1st battalion, this meant soldiering in India between 1857 and 1870 followed by a period of home service which lasted until 1878. Malta was the next overseas station, and the battalion returned to the West Indies in 1883 before being sent to Africa for the first time in the battalion's history (the 2nd battalion had already served in Egypt, in 1801–02). Between 1884 and 1891 it took part in a number of operations in southern Africa – Bechuanaland, Cape Colony, Natal and Zululand – before returning to Britain for six years.

The 2nd battalion was also regularly on the move. In 1858 it sailed for Hong Kong, another first, and took part in offensive operations in China during the Second Opium War, which began when the Chinese authorities seized the British ship *Arrow*. Following the capture of Canton by a joint British and French force under the command of Admiral Sir Michael Seymour, the Taku forts near Tientsin were attacked from the sea. In the early summer of 1860 the 2nd battalion took part in amphibious operations to land at Pei-tang at the mouth of the Peiho River, and the forts at Taku were taken by assault with the help of a naval flotilla. This opened the way to Peking, which fell after two sharp actions which resulted in the defeat of a Chinese army which was 30,000-strong and twice the size of the British force. Peking and its Summer Palace were subsequently sacked in revenge for the death and mutilation of a British peace delegation led by Sir Harry Smith Parkes. At the end of the year the Royals were back in Britain, where a short period at home was followed by a further deployment in India which lasted from 1866 to 1880. This meant that for four years both of the regiment's battalions were stationed in the sub-continent. The 2nd battalion then spent ten years in Britain largely supplying drafts for the 1st battalion, but by 1892 it was back in India.

The movements of the Royals' two battalions between 1872 and 1881 reflect the attempts made by the army to bring some much-needed cohesion to its recruiting strategies as the nineteenth century drew to a close. During the stewardship of Edward Cardwell as Secretary for War, the infantry was reformed by the Localisation Bill of 1872. Under its terms the country was divided into sixty-six regimental districts, each one containing a regiment with two line battalions, a militia battalion and a depot to handle the management of the regiment's recruits and serving soldiers. Driving the reform was the theory that one battalion would serve at home while the other was stationed abroad and would receive drafts and reliefs from the home-based battalion to keep it up to strength. Nine years later, in 1881, the system was completed by

Cardwell's successor, Hugh Childers, with the permanent linking of the regular and auxiliary battalions. Because The Royal Scots was already a two-battalion regiment, the Cardwell/Childers reforms were easily embraced. As a result of the localisation changes regimental numbers disappeared and territorial names were adopted. In the first instance the Royals became The Lothian Regiment (Royal Scots), but this was quickly changed to The Royal Scots (Lothian Regiment). A more enduring adjustment was the creation of the regiment's 3rd battalion from the Edinburgh Light Infantry Militia and the establishment of a permanent depot at Glencorse, near Penicuik to the south of Edinburgh. To cement the regiment's return to its Scottish roots the Royals started wearing tartan trews of the government, or 'Black Watch', tartan and a forage cap with a red and white diced border.

The changes were as heatedly debated as any reforms – the loss of regimental numbers was particularly lamented by older soldiers – but they did have a lasting effect on the future structure of the infantry. Regiments now had recognised territorial associations, which last to the present day, and although localisation was not the complete answer to the army's recruiting problems, the new system did help to cement links with the local community. In the Royals' case this meant that its hinterland was the city of Edinburgh and the counties of the Lothians. In theory the arrangement should have worked, but like so many reforms in the history of the British Army, the practice was quickly overtaken by events. Shortly after the regimental reforms had been introduced the army had to find additional forces to fight in Africa – in the Ashanti War of 1873–74 and the Zulu War of 1879. As a result of these and other existing commitments the numbers did not stack up and by 1879 there were 82 infantry battalions serving abroad with only 59 at home to support them. (The imbalance was caused by the Queen's Own Cameron Highlanders, which had only one battalion until 1897.) For the Royals the arrangement meant that the 1ˢᵗ battalion was the home-based battalion from 1870 until 1878, while the 2ⁿᵈ battalion took over those duties in 1880. In both cases the battalions found that the system of supplying drafts had an adverse effect on morale and unit cohesion, not least because India was a popular posting and men were unwilling to come home at the end of a deployment. On leaving India in 1870 over 300 men from the 1ˢᵗ battalion volunteered to stay on in the country, offering to serve in other regiments.

In all, the Royals spent a total of 64 years serving in India, or the 'Shiny' as the soldiers of the late Victorian army often called the country. Until India became independent in 1947 following the partition with Pakistan, it was very much a home-from-home for regiments like The Royal Scots. Compared with service in the United Kingdom, life in India for a soldier was 'cushy'. Even the youngest or most recently enlisted private was treated as a 'sahib', although as Richard Holmes has pointed out in his history of soldiering in India, they were also referred to less politely as '*gora log* [Europeans], red of face and coat, intent on mischief in the bazaar'. Whatever their title, British soldiers were generally excused the kind of chores which would have been given to them at home in Britain. Cleaning up barracks was left to the sweepers, Indians did all the work in the cookhouse, and the laundry was in the hands of the washerwomen. In return, a number of words entered the soldiers' vocabulary to be anglicised and used wherever a regiment was posted – *buckshee* (free, gratis), *charpoy* (bed), *chit* (written message), *jeldi* (hurry up), *pukka* (proper), *tiffin* (lunch or midday meal). Many can still be heard being used by British soldiers in the twenty-first century. Another innovation was the use of lighter clothes, and by the 1880s khaki was in widespread use, although as Frank Richards of The Royal Welch Fusiliers remembered in his memoir, *Old Soldier. Sahib*, it proved difficult for soldiers to abandon altogether their time-honoured uniforms:

> On the Plains and in the winter we wore thin, fine Indian khaki by day and red in the evening: I think that a suit of red was supposed to last us two years. The red Indian jacket was lighter than the home service one; and we were not issued with red tunics. During the heat of summer on the Plains we always wore white on parades – but as the only parades then were Church Parades and funerals this was seldom. In the Hills during these months we wore the Indian khaki.

Apart from taking part in internal security duties or fighting the occasional war on the frontier, the pattern of service for most soldiers was undemanding and mostly pleasant. Due to the excessive heat, especially during the dry season (April to October), all parades were over by mid-morning and there was no further activity until the cool of the evening. Route marches along India's long and grimy roads were a regular feature of military life and although they were tedious, as Lieutenant William Hodson argued in his persuasive memoirs of the years before the Mutiny of 1857, most soldiers came to terms with the heat and the dust and even came to admire the ever-changing scenery as the regiment marched across the expanse of India:

> Soon after 4 a.m. the bugle sounds the reveille and the whole mass is astir at once. The smoke of the evening fires has by this time blown away and everything stands out clear and defined in the moonlight. The sepoys [Indian soldiers] bring the straw from their tents and make fires to warm their faces on all sides and the groups of swarthy

redcoats stooping over the blaze with a white background of canvas and the dark clear sky behind all produces a most picturesque effect as one turns out into the cold. The multitude of camels, horses and elephants, in all imaginable groups and positions – the groans and cries of the former as they stoop and kneel for their burdens, the neighing of hundreds of horses mingling with the shouts of the innumerable servants and their masters' calls, the bleating of the sheep and goats, and louder than all, the shrill screams of the Hindoo women, almost bedevil one's senses as one treads one's way through the canvas streets and squares to the place where the regiment assembles outside the camp.

Once experienced – India is a country which assaults all the senses, often simultaneously – men never forgot the country or its fantastic sights, sounds and smells. During their time in India both battalions of the Royals had ample opportunity to come into contact with the place in all its varying moods and to enjoy the sensations described by young Hodson. (Later, he went on to raise his own irregular cavalry regiment, known as Hodson's Horse.) During their deployment after the Crimean War, the 1st battalion was based in southern India, including a spell at Masulipatam, a Dutch-built fort outside Madras (modern Chennai) which was so damp and unhealthy that 'a frog or an alligator would have chosen it for its habitation'. One regiment based there in the 1830s had to ban the playing of the 'Dead March' as its repetitious strains had a depressing effect on the patients in the garrison hospital. In one year alone the Royals lost 105 men to dysentery. It helped that regimental wives accompanied the battalion and often worked as auxiliary nurses, but there was a downside to their presence. Like the men, the wives also enjoyed better conditions than they would have done at home in Britain – purpose-built bungalows were supplied for families – but, as the writer Maud Diver recalled in her account, *British Women in India,* they 'became camp equipment, jolted in bullock-carts and on the backs of camels, exposed to dust, sun, heat, cholera and malaria, moving always from tent to bungalow and back again, gypsies without a home, hearth beneath the stars'.

For the 2nd battalion, India meant the north-west of the country but in 1895 they renewed their acquaintance with Burma, being stationed there for four years on internal security duties in Mandalay. In the years since the Royals had first been in Burma there had been a process of gradual territorial annexation, with wars in 1852–53 and 1885–87. On their return to India in 1899 the battalion was based in Poona, the hot weather station for Bombay, which fully lived up to the ironic description that India was simply a vast place of outdoor recreation for British soldiers. A glimpse at the regimental magazine *The Thistle* (first published in 1893) confirms that the battalion enjoyed the whole range of sports which were on offer, as well as taking part in the obligatory military manoeuvres and exercises. The Royals were in Poona until 1903 before returning to Britain in 1909 following their last posting in Bombay. By then Britain had been engaged in a major conflict in South Africa – the Boer War – which lasted from 1899 to 1902.

With the 2nd battalion stationed in India it fell to the 1st battalion to represent the regiment in a conflict which proved to be the costliest and most humiliating war fought by Britain between Waterloo and the outbreak of the First World War in 1914. Britain had been at loggerheads with the Boers – Dutch immigrants who had settled in Cape Colony – for most of the century. Even when the Boers began trekking north to establish Transvaal and the Orange Free State in 1837 the confrontation continued and broke out into open war in 1880 as a result of non-payment of taxes. Following the humiliating defeat of a British force at Majuba Hill, an uneasy peace was restored, with the Boers operating self-government under British suzerainty, but it was a powder keg awaiting the spark. The spark was provided by the discovery of seemingly limitless supplies of gold in the Witwatersrand ridge, also known as the 'Rand', south of Pretoria. The lure of untold riches attracted speculators from Britain and all over Europe and before long the Boers were outnumbered by foreigners or *uitlanders* who threatened their traditional conservative way of life. To protect his fellow Boers in the Transvaal President Kruger passed stringent laws excluding non-Boers from participation in political life while retaining the right to tax them.

Such an awkward state of affairs was bound to cause trouble, but when it came in 1895 it proved to be a botched business. Acting in the belief that an *uitlander* uprising was imminent the British imperial adventurer, Cecil Rhodes, encouraged his associate, Dr Starr Jameson, to lead a raid into the Transvaal to bring down Kruger's government. It was an abject failure, but it had far-reaching consequences. Rhodes was disgraced and Britain was made a laughing stock, and to make matters worse, the subsequent negotiations to retrieve the situation settled nothing. Each new concession was met with further demands and gradually a full-scale war became inevitable. In 1899 Britain dispatched 10,000 troops to South Africa while the Transvaal, now backed by the Orange Free State, made plans for mobilisation. War was declared on 12 October after Kruger's demands that Britain remove its troops from the frontier were contemptuously ignored in London, and within a week General Sir Redvers Buller VC, one of the country's foremost soldiers, was on his way to South Africa to take command of the imperial forces in what everyone hoped would be a short sharp war. He was given a hero's send-off when he boarded the RMS *Dunnottar Castle* at Southampton and the slightly hysterical mood surrounding his departure was captured by a cartoon in *Punch* that same week. It showed two London street urchins discussing the forthcoming conflict. 'The Boers will cop it now,' one tells the other. 'Farfer's gone to South Africa, an' tooken 'is strap!'

The Royals were amongst the first regiments to arrive in South Africa, where the 1st battalion became part of the hastily improvised 3rd Division commanded by Lieutenant-General Sir William Gatacre, who had served in the Omdurman campaign in the Sudan earlier in the decade. Known throughout the army as 'Back-acher', following an astonishing manoeuvre when he marched his brigade 130 miles in 6 days to join Kitchener's army in time to take part in the Battle of the Atbara in 1898, Gatacre was a solid if somewhat uninspired commander who proved to be slow in adapting to the new conditions of warfare in South Africa and placed too much reliance on his soldiers' supposed racial superiority. To most people at home in Britain the task facing Buller and his regiments seemed to be simple enough, and if past form were anything to go by the Boers would be defeated before Christmas. British soldiers were part of the most professional army in the world and they were fighting against Boer forces which seemed to be little more than a makeshift citizens' militia. In the event, though, the fighting was to last almost three years, the Boers were to gain some notable victories and Britain's eventual victory was to require rather more effort than the simple wielding of 'Farfer's strap'.

For the 1st battalion the first intimation of trouble came a week before the declaration of war, when it received its mobilisation papers at its base in Belfast. For the first time, the reservists were

called up and started arriving in Northern Ireland by the end
of the month and the battalion started moving out on 4 and 5
November. For the first time, too, the battalion was ordered to
provide a mounted section, which would become part of a new
force of 20,000 Mounted Infantry (MI) troopers. These were
ordered by the War Office as 'a matter of immediate urgency and
permanent importance' and were supposed to 'shoot as well as
possible and ride decently'. Acting as scouts and rapid-response
forces, they were to be one of the more successful innovations
of the war. The majority came from dominion forces and
from British yeomanry regiments, but at least a quarter of the
number was raised from regular battalions – all told, the Royals
supplied three and a half companies of just under four hundred
MI troopers, most of whom were reservists with experience of
horses. Rudyard Kipling captured something of their irregular or
'scallywag' nature in his poem 'M.I.':

> That is what we are known as – we are the push you
> require
> For outposts all night under freezin', and rearguard all
> day under fire.
> Anything 'ot or unwholesome? Anything dusty or dry?
> Borrow a bunch of Ikonas! Trot out the old M.I.

The Royals' MI section departed ahead of the battalion, which
arrived at East London on 4 December and immediately joined
Gatacre's forces.

Two months later reinforcements arrived in the shape of the 3rd
(Militia) battalion which had been embodied for war service on the
1st battalion's departure and immediately moved from Glencorse
to Belfast. Having agreed to volunteer for war service, they left
for South Africa on 28 March 1900 and provided much-needed

support to the regular army, as did many other militia battalions during the conflict. All told, 45,000 militia soldiers saw war service in South Africa. Militiamen had always served in the British Army as a defence force, originally selected by ballot, but it had often proved to be a mixed blessing. In 1852 a new act put the force on a sounder footing. While recruits continued to be volunteers, they could transfer to the regular army after three months' training or decide to stay on as part-time soldiers provided they agreed to train for a month in every year. To give coherence to the scheme, under the Cardwell/Childers reforms militia battalions were linked to the regular battalions of their parent regiment. Before the men of the 3rd battalion were asked to volunteer for service in South Africa they received strict instructions from the Inspector General of Recruiting and Auxiliary Forces, Major-General H.C. Borrett, about the limits of the service that was expected of them:

> Very strict orders were given to generals to the effect that in every district where a regiment was going abroad the general should personally see it on parade, and ask the men whether they quite understood the terms, that there was no compulsion, that everything was quite voluntary and that if any man did not wish to go no questions would be asked. It was entirely voluntary and that was all carried out right through.

It is a testimony to the *esprit de corps* within The Royal Scots that 21 officers and 579 men of the 3rd battalion volunteered for overseas service. Most of their service was spent on garrison and lines of communication duties and the battalion did not return home until May 1902, having spent two and a half years in South Africa.

Within weeks of arriving in South Africa the Royals were in

action, as Boer forces began invading Cape Colony from their positions in the Orange Free State. This was the first phase of the war and it lasted from October 1899 to February 1900. For the British it was also the most disastrous stage of the conflict: the Boers began the investment of the key positions at Ladysmith, Mafeking and Kimberley and a series of military blunders led to heavy defeats at Stormberg, Magersfontein and Colenso, the latter setbacks happening in the course of what came to be known as 'Black Week'. The first disaster occurred on 10 December, when Gatacre led his division to capture the strategically important railway junction at Stormberg. Having embarked on a night march the men then got lost and found themselves moving in the wrong direction, and were promptly set upon by the well-rested Boers. Lacking clear orders, the British infantrymen were forced to retire towards the nearest railway station at Molteno, which was held by a reserve including two companies of the 1st Royal Scots. Despite putting up a brave fight, Gatacre's division lost almost 700 men, most of them from The Northumberland Fusiliers, who found themselves isolated and were forced to surrender.

The defeats led to a radical reappraisal of the army's role in South Africa. Buller was sacked and in his place command was given to Lord Roberts, who had won the Victoria Cross during the Indian Mutiny of 1857 and who had come to national prominence during the campaigning in Afghanistan in 1878–80. With him, as Chief of Staff and virtual second-in-command, went Lord Kitchener of Khartoum, the victor of Omdurman and one of the great icons of Britain's imperial history. They were very different in personality and military background – a contemporary described Roberts as a 'modern Bayard' whereas Kitchener was 'fashioned more on the lines of Bismarck' – but between them, they were to turn the tide of the war and pave the way to eventual victory. At the beginning of January 1900 they were in South Africa and struck back quickly and effectively against the Boers by sweeping them out into the open country so that the cavalry could 'make an example of them'. In quick succession Kitchener defeated the Boers at Paardeberg, and the siege of Ladysmith was lifted, the latter even happily taking place on 27 February, the nineteenth anniversary of Majuba Hill. This was the turning point and the war entered a new phase with the invasion of the Orange Free State and the Transvaal. By September Pretoria and Johannesburg had been occupied, the Boer army under Commandant-General Martinus Prinsloo had capitulated at Brandwater Basin and Kruger had been forced to take flight to Europe.

During this phase of the war the Royals took part in the invasion of Transvaal, and the subsequent mopping-up operations along the mountainous border with Mozambique. Although casualties were light throughout 1900 the operations against the Boers were far from easy. The going on the veldt was hard, with long route marches under the hot sun, and nights spent on the veldt, where temperatures plummeted during the hours of darkness. A brief diary entry by Private Watters of the 1st battalion gives some idea of the privations he and his fellow soldiers endured while pursuing the Boers south of Bloemfontein in March:

> We arrived next day at Kraal Ferriera, and were marched
> to a Kopje, where after digging our trenches, we had to
> lie down with all our equipment on, and our rifles by our
> sides, awaiting an attack, which never came.

Most old soldiers will recognise the resigned fatalism in Watters's words. Life for the Royals, as for every other soldier fighting on the veldt, was a mixture of discomfort and boredom interspersed by orders to move quickly and then stand down, all the while under the ever-present threat of engaging the Boers. At the end of the summer the 1ˢᵗ battalion was based at Koomatipoort on the Mozambique border before moving to Barberton on the border with present-day Somaliland.

To all intents and purposes the war should have been over. The main Boer strongholds were in British possession, the lines of communication had been secured and the Boer leadership was fractured, but the war was destined to last another 18 months in its third and final phase. At the end of the year Roberts handed over command to Kitchener, but instead of tying up the loose ends he found himself engaged in a lengthy and bitter guerrilla war with an enemy who refused to give up the fight. Before leaving South Africa, Roberts described the Boers as 'a few marauding bands', but he had under-estimated their strength and determination. In fact, some 30,000 Boer guerrillas were still in the field and they cared little that their major cities had been captured. Their loss did not signal the end of nationhood. As long as they had rifles and ammunition and a sense of burning loyalty to the Boer cause they pledged to continue the fight. As soldiers, they understood that the numerical superiority of the British Army made outright victory impossible, but they took heart from its over-stretched lines of communication and the sheer size of their country. Most of the veldt was still free and the guerrillas made it their home, using deception, speed and marksmanship in place of fortification and artillery. Some areas, such as the western Transvaal and Zoutspanberg to the north, were never captured at all.

With his army stretched out along the main lines of communication, Kitchener decided to turn the position to his own advantage. He began by ordering a series of drives across the country to sweep the Boers out of their hiding places. Everything in the path of the advancing infantry had to be destroyed, with the result that the army found itself facing large marauding gangs of farmers, plus their women and children, swarming over the blackened remains of a ruined countryside. His solution to that problem was to house the dispossessed, and the families of Boers who had surrendered, in protected camps alongside the main railway lines until the hostilities came to an end. The camps were run on military lines and basic rations and accommodation were provided but the formation of these 'concentration camps' (as they were known) caused great outrage. Kitchener claimed that he had solved the problem of a rootless population, but he paid little attention to the proper provision of the camps; people were herded together in barbaric conditions, rations were basic and medical supplies were non-existent. Later, it was found that 20,000 Boers died in the camps, either from disease or malnutrition, and the camps' existence became a source of great bitterness in the years to come.

Nonetheless, from a military point of view Kitchener's tactics did work. Once housed in the camps the local population could not help the guerrillas in the field, and the sweeps and drives helped to round up large numbers of Boer fighters. The policy was helped by the construction of block-houses linked by wire fences, which compartmentalised the countryside and removed the Boers' greatest assets – mobility and the ability to melt away into the hidden reaches of the veldt. It was a time-consuming exercise which tried the patience and endurance of the British Army. Although success was described in shooting terms as 'Boers in the bag', the terrain militated against the methods and huge effort might be rewarded only by a handful of prisoners and greater numbers of cattle and oxen. The 1st battalion took part in several operations throughout 1901, but its records show that it had a lean time. At the end of April it raided a Boer *laager* at Goedhoop but only managed to capture four Boers and nine rifles plus ammunition. Its agricultural bag was somewhat better: 553 cattle, 2,433 sheep and 75 horses; in the same operation the battalion lost one soldier killed and seven wounded. The battalion's diary of a sweep and drive in mid–May records in stark terms the difficulties and dangers of these far from simple operations:

> The Bermondsey position consisted of a hill, the top of which was covered with large rocks; the enemy's left rested on a precipice; immediately in front of his position was a deep gully in front of which a line of rocks jutted out at right angles to the enemy's front. In these advanced rocks, which lay on the right of the column's line of advance, Boers were concealed, and they did not disclose themselves until the MI scouts were within a few yards of them, when they opened a hot fire from their main and advanced position; the two companies of the battalion forming an advanced guard pushed on.

It was the same story for the rest of the war which eventually drew to a close in the spring of 1902, and was concluded by the signing of the Treaty of Vereeniging. During that summer the regiment's reservists were demobilised, but the battalion did not return to Britain until the following March, when it was stationed at Blackdown in the south of England.

Once again, the experience of a major war had an effect on defence expenditure and the management of the armed forces, only on this occasion the fighting in South Africa had revealed the uncomfortable truth that Britain and its empire were not an unassailable force. Once that had been understood it was obvious that the army had to change, and that radical reform was needed to improve its performance. One result was the creation of the Territorial Force, which was established for home defence in 1908 and was composed of part-time soldiers who volunteered to train once a week in addition to a fortnight's camp. For the infantry the Territorial soldiers served in their own battalions, which were an integral part of the regiment and numbered accordingly. For The Royal Scots the regular element was provided by the 1st and 2nd battalions followed by the Militia (Special Reserve) battalion at the depot and then came the new Territorial Force battalions in the following sequence:

4th (Queen's Edinburgh) battalion. This was formed from the 1st Edinburgh (City) Rifle Volunteer Corps which had been founded in 1859. In 1867 it became the 1st battalion of the Queen's City of Edinburgh Rifle Volunteer Brigade and joined The Royal Scots in the reforms of 1881.

5th (Queen's Edinburgh) battalion. This was formed from the 2nd battalion of the Queen's City of Edinburgh Rifle Volunteer Brigade.

6th battalion. Formed from Number 16 Company of the 1st Edinburgh (City) Rifle Volunteer Corps which was raised by total abstainers and members of the British Temperance League. In 1867 it became the 3rd battalion of the Edinburgh (City) Rifle Volunteer Corps and in 1888 became the 4th Volunteer Battalion, Royal Scots.

7th battalion. Formed originally from the four companies of the 1st Midlothian Rifle Volunteer Corps which were raised in Leith in 1859. In 1888 it became the 5th Volunteer Battalion, Royal Scots.

8th battalion. Formed in 1908 by the amalgamation of the old 6th and 7th Volunteer Battalions, Royal Scots, which recruited in Midlothian and Peeblesshire.

9th (Highlanders) battalion. Formed as the 'Highland'

battalion of the Queen's City of Edinburgh Rifle
Volunteer Brigade during the Boer War. In 1900 it
became 9th (Highlanders) Volunteer Battalion, Royal
Scots. Locally it was known as the 'Dandy Ninth'.

10th (Cyclist) battalion. Formed originally from the
1st Admin Battalion of the Linlithgowshire Rifle
Volunteers it became the 8th Volunteer Battalion, Royal
Scots in 1888 and was re-designated 10th (Cyclist)
Battalion in 1908.

Most of the volunteer battalions had provided the army with
reinforcements during the fighting in South Africa and were
considered to be an integral part of the Royals' regimental family.
The reforms also affected the regular army which was re-formed
into two corps, each one consisting of two divisions. Each division
was made up of four brigades composed of four infantry battalions
and the whole would provide the basis for a new expeditionary
force in the event of an overseas war involving Britain. For the
first time, too, detailed official manuals were produced for the
organisation and training of the army and the mobilisation of
the expeditionary force. When the 2nd battalion returned from
India in 1909 it was initially based in Scotland before moving to
Plymouth three years later, where it became part of 8th Brigade in
the 3rd Division. For the whole regiment there had also been other
important changes. In place of the trews of government tartan
which had been worn for the past 20 years the Royals received
permission to wear trews in Hunting Stuart tartan. Another
feature was the introduction of the broad flat Kilmarnock bonnet,
which helped to give the regiment a more distinctive Scottish
appearance.

The new twentieth century had begun with a war which,
in Kipling's words, had taught Britain 'no end of a lesson'.

Fortunately the warnings had been heeded and the necessary steps had been taken to ensure that the country once again had an army worthy of the name. As events in Europe soon showed, the reforms had been introduced not a moment too soon.

SIX

THE FIRST WORLD WAR: THE WESTERN FRONT

In the summer of 1914 the long European peace was shattered when a series of connected events led the great powers to mobilise their armed forces and begin a global conflict. It was known at the time as the Great War and, later, as the First World War. The chain of events began on 28 June, when the heir to the throne of Austria-Hungary, Archduke Franz Ferdinand, was assassinated together with his wife in Sarajevo, the capital of the province of Bosnia-Herzegovina. Initially, the incident seemed to be an isolated terrorist attack and the first reaction was that the perpetrators would be caught and punished by the imperial authorities. Even when it was reported that the blame for the outrage was being shifted onto neighbouring Serbia, the first of the Slav states to gain independence in the Balkans and a source of constant irritation in Vienna, there was no reason to believe that the incident would precipitate a crisis. In Scotland and elsewhere the general opinion was that even if there was a war it would only be a local affair involving the two countries. However, the killings had lit a slow-burning fuse: the assassin Gavrilo Princip had links to a Serbian nationalist group called the Black Hand, which in turn was supported by Serbian military intelligence, and it did not take long for anti-Serb sentiment to sweep through Austria-Hungary, creating a mood for revenge.

What followed next was the well-documented progression towards global confrontation, with demands being issued, threats being made and positions becoming entrenched as Europe marched inexorably towards war. The first flashpoint came on 23 July, when Austria-Hungary issued an ultimatum to Serbia, making ten demands for the suppression of Serb nationalist groups, the punishment of the assassins and participation in the judicial process. Serbia was given 48 hours to comply, but stopped short of allowing Austria-Hungary to take part in the trial of Princip and his associates, arguing that it should be referred to the International Court at The Hague. The response seemed sufficient to avert a wider crisis, but already diplomacy was proving powerless to stop Europe's drift towards war. Both countries mobilised their armed forces as Germany, Austria-Hungary's main ally, encouraged Vienna to take decisive action against the Serbs before any other country intervened in the crisis. On 28 July, confident of German support, Austria-Hungary declared war on Serbia and the European house of cards began to collapse. The following day, Russia, Serbia's traditional friend and protector, began to mobilise its forces along the border with Austria-Hungary, and within 24 hours this was followed by the order for full mobilisation.

Although the move was made to discourage Austria-Hungary, it threatened Germany, which immediately demanded that Russia 'cease every war measure against us and Austria-Hungary'. On 1 August Germany declared war on Russia, followed two days later by a further declaration of war against France, Russia's ally.

That same day German forces began crossing into Belgium as part of a pre-arranged plan called the Schlieffen Plan, to bypass the heavily-fortified French frontier and encircle Paris from the north through Belgium. Britain was not formally in alliance with any of the main participants, but was now about to be pressed into the conflict through a treaty of 1839, which guaranteed Belgium's neutrality. On 4 August, having received no answer to an ultimatum that there must be no attack on Belgium, Britain declared war on Germany.

From a military perspective, Britain's first strategic move was to mobilise the regular army and as part of the 'Precautionary Period' of the Defence Plan Prior to Mobilisation, formations of the regular army based in Britain were told to return to their depots on 29 July. Most were on their annual summer camps or were involved in training exercises = at the end of July the 2nd battalion was taking part in a field firing exercise with 8th Brigade, when it was ordered to return to Plymouth in preparation for mobilisation. At the same time, some 500 reservists were processed by the regimental depot for service with the Royals. As one of their number remembered, the system worked with cool efficiency: on the morning of 5 August, having said his farewells to his wife and family, he left his home in Musselburgh by train and was not at all surprised to find other Royal Scots joining him before they arrived at the regimental depot at Glencorse:

> I reported myself at the guardroom, and the sergeant, after taking all particulars, gave me a form and directed me to the hospital to go before the doctor. I wasn't long in his hands, and being fit and sound, I was told to go over to the Orderly Room to pass before the Commanding Officer. At the same time I was to hand in my old discharge papers. That done, the next move was towards the Keep. There I

got my kit and equipment, all bundled into a blanket, and
with these thrown over my shoulder and my rifle in hand,
I marched to the drill shed, which was our temporary
quarters, changed my clothes, and lo and behold, there
I was, a soldier once again. The whole proceedings only
took about an hour all told, as everything was ready. It
was just a case of in one door a civilian and out the other
a soldier.

The anonymous diarist in the 2nd battalion and his fellow reservists
were then sent by train to Plymouth that same night. Earlier in
the day he had told his wife that he might be home again in three
weeks, and if he had to stay at Glencorse she and the children
would be able to visit him. In common with many others, he
thought that the fighting would be over by Christmas.

At the same time, steps were taken to bring back from India
the regular battalions which were serving in the country, and on
16 November the 1st battalion arrived back in England, where
it joined 81st Brigade in 27th Division. By then, Kitchener had
joined the government as Secretary of War and had astounded
his Cabinet colleagues by declaring that the conflict would last
three years and Britain would need 1,000,000 men to win it.
As a result, the British Army began to expand dramatically to
meet the need for men, and two other armies came into being to
support the regulars – the Territorial Force battalions and the
Special Service battalions of the 'New' or 'Kitchener' armies,
both of which would be linked to the army's existing infantry
regiments. The rapid growth of the army meant that The Royal
Scots expanded massively during the course of the war and
eventually raised 35 battalions. All played a leading role, from
seeing active service to raising and training soldiers at home
in Scotland, England or Ireland. By the war's end in 1918 the

regiment was made up in the following way and served on the fronts as indicated:

1st Battalion (Regular Army) – Western Front, Salonika, Russia

2nd Battalion (Regular Army) – Western Front

3rd (Reserve) Battalion (Regular Army) – Scotland, England, Ireland

1/4th (Queen's Edinburgh Rifles) Battalion (Territorial Force) – Gallipoli, Egypt, Palestine

2/4th (Queen's Edinburgh Rifles) Battalion (Territorial Force) – Scotland, Essex, Ireland

3/4th (Queen's Edinburgh Rifles) Battalion (Territorial Force) – Scotland

4th (Reserve) Battalion (Territorial Force) – Scotland, Catterick

1/5th (Queen's Edinburgh Rifles) Battalion (Territorial Force) – Gallipoli, Egypt, France

2/5th (Queen's Edinburgh Rifles) Battalion (Territorial Force) – Scotland

3/5th (Queen's Edinburgh Rifles) Battalion (Territorial Force) – Scotland

1/6th Battalion (Territorial Force) – coastal defence Scotland, North Africa, France

2/6th Battalion (Territorial Force) – Scotland

3/6th Battalion (Territorial Force) – Scotland

5/6th Battalion (Territorial Force) – Western Front (formed in 1916 from 1/5th and 1/6th Battalions)

1/7th Battalion (Territorial Force) – Gallipoli, Egypt, Palestine

2/7th Battalion (Territorial Force) coastal defence Scotland, Essex, Ireland

3/7th Battalion (Territorial Force) – Scotland

1/8th Battalion (Territorial Force) – Western Front

2/8th Battalion (Territorial Force) – Scotland, Essex

3/8th Battalion (Territorial Force) – Scotland

1/9th (Highlanders) Battalion (Territorial Force) – Western Front

2/9th (Highlanders) Battalion (Territorial Force) – Scotland, Essex

3/9th (Highlanders) Battalion (Territorial Force) – Scotland, Catterick

1/10th (Cyclist) Battalion (Territorial Force) – Scotland, Ireland

2/10th (Cyclist) Battalion (Territorial Force) – coastal defence Scotland, Ireland, Aldershot, Russia

11th Battalion (New Army) – Western Front

12th Battalion (New Army) – Western Front

13th Battalion (New Army) – Western Front

14th (Reserve) Battalion (New Army) – Scotland

15th (Cranston's, 1st City of Edinburgh) Battalion (New Army) – Western Front

16th (McCrae's, 2nd City of Edinburgh) Battalion (New Army) – Western Front

17th (Rosebery's Bantams) Battalion (New Army) – Western Front

18th (Reserve) Battalion (New Army) – England

19th (Labour) Battalion (Mixed) – Scotland, France

1st Garrison Battalion (Mixed) – Mudros, Egypt, Cyprus

2nd Garrison Battalion (Mixed) – Scotland

The Royal Scots' make-up and its experiences during the war were not untypical, and from the regiment's order of battle a pattern emerges. Both the regular battalions saw action, as did the first battalion of each of the Territorial Force formations and all but the 14th Battalion of the New Army formations. Two battalions (1st and 2/10th) served in Russia in 1919 during the operations against Bolshevik forces, and the regiment fought on every battle front except Mesopotamia and East and West Africa.

One of the most popular manifestations of the volunteering craze in that unreal late summer and autumn of 1914 was the formation of 'pals' battalions – so-called because they kept together volunteers from the same cities or towns, or from working, sporting or social clubs. All told, 215 'pals', or locally raised, battalions had been formed by the summer of 1916 and although the title was never fully recognised in Scotland, the concept of men serving together did catch on, especially in the big cities. Shortly after the declaration of war, three distinctive volunteer battalions of the Highland Light Infantry were formed with men from the city's Tramways Department, Glasgow Boys' Brigade and the Glasgow Chamber of Commerce. Not to be outdone, Edinburgh also followed suit. The first calls for a regiment of city volunteers appeared in *The Scotsman* on 12 August, but it was not until 12 September that Lord Provost Robert Kirk Inches announced that a 'City of Edinburgh Battalion' would be formed. By then the local regiment, The Royal Scots, had formed three service battalions for the New Armies (11th, 12th, 13th) but Inches was keen to see a designated Edinburgh regiment which would be the equal of the three Glasgow battalions. The result was the formation of two battalions which served with The Royal Scots as, respectively 15th (1st City of Edinburgh, Service) and 16th (2nd City of Edinburgh, Service). As they both owed their existence to local commanding officers, they were also known by the men who served in them as Cranston's Battalion and McCrae's Battalion.

Both men were prominent members of the local business community. Sir Robert Cranston had served as treasurer and provost on the city council and had interests in local drapery stores and temperance hotels, and like many of his class he enjoyed a long association with the old Volunteer movement. Sir George McCrae was equally well regarded but he was a self-made man who had set up in the drapery business on his own account, having managed to bury the secret that he had been born an illegitimate child, a fact that could have hindered his advancement. Hard work had made him a wealthy man and he was elected to parliament as a Liberal MP in 1899; like Cranston he also served as a Volunteer. Both battalions were raised in the latter months of 1914, and both went on to serve on the Western Front, but McCrae's battalion was unique in that it contained a large number of footballers, most of whom played for one of the local football clubs, the romantically named Heart of Midlothian. Shortly after the battalion was raised, one of the new recruits penned a suitable verse for McCrae to read out when he appeared in uniform at a special performance of the annual Christmas pantomime in the King's Theatre: 'Do not ask where Hearts are playing and then look at me askance. If it's football that you're wanting, you must come with us to France.' By then McCrae had recruited over 1,000 officers and men, and his battalion assembled in George Street on 15 December, with each volunteer being told to bring with him 'one pair good Boots, Topcoat, two pairs Socks, and shaving outfit'. The occasion prompted a good deal of local excitement when they marched off to their temporary billets in the Examination Halls of George Heriot's School and the nearby Castle Brewery. Their story is movingly told in Jack Alexander's history *McCrae's Battalion*.

1914

Being one of the first formations of the British Expeditionary Force (BEF) to serve in France, the 2nd battalion was the first to see action, at the end of August, in II Corps' operations to support the French Fifth Army during the advance into Belgium. The expected German assault began on the morning of 23 August and for the attacking enemy infantrymen it was a sobering experience. Trained to fire 15 rifle rounds a minute, the infantrymen of the British regiments poured their fire into the advancing German lines, with predictable results – the rate was so rapid and concentrated that the Germans believed they were facing machine-gun fire. During their attack on the 2nd battalion's positions on the Mons–Harmingies road, the 75th Regiment lost 381 soldiers, while the defenders' casualties were slight – one officer and one soldier wounded and four others reported missing. By the end of the day the attack had faltered, as exhausted and frightened Germans attempted to regroup, but despite halting the assault the BEF was obliged to retire, and in the coming days its regiments were to receive increasingly high casualties. At one point in the British retreat, D Company, 2nd Royal Scots, was reduced to one officer and seventeen soldiers and the battalion lost its commanding officer, Lieutenant-Colonel McMicking.

The Great Retreat towards the River Marne, as it was known, would take the German army to the outskirts of Paris, and the BEF suffered further casualties on 26 August when II Corps turned to face the advancing Germans at Le Cateau some 30 miles from Mons. It was the British Army's biggest set-piece battle since Waterloo and its 55,000 soldiers faced German opposition which numbered 140,000. General Sir Horace Smith-Dorrien's three divisions, supported by the Cavalry Division, were able to hold the line by dint of their superior firepower, but by evening they were outnumbered and only a German failure to press home their advantage allowed II Corps to resume their retreat. Even so, the casualties were heavy – 7,812 killed – and gave a stark indication of worse things to come. Ahead lay the Battle of the Aisne, fought on 13 September, where the British were able to consolidate and counter-attack to good effect.

The fighting marked a new phase of the operations and signalled the end of a war of manoeuvre as both sides struggled to fill the gap between the Aisne and the Channel coast before it was exploited. This was known as the 'Race for the Sea', and it ended in stalemate, with the only potential gap in the line being the wastes of the Flanders plain, an unprepossessing region peppered with names which soon became drearily familiar to the soldiers who fought over it – Ypres, Passchendaele, Messines, Langemarck, Vimy, Arras. The style of the fighting was also changing, as the armies faced one another in the fields of Flanders. Trenches were dug, barbed-wire obstacles were thrown up and field fortifications constructed; the German plan to encircle Paris had finally been blunted in the mud of Flanders and the first great set-piece battles were about to be fought. The town of Ypres was the fulcrum of the German attempt to break through and the first battle was fought there between 20 October and 22 November. For the British it was the first great killing battle of the war. Although the BEF stemmed the German attack, it paid a heavy price: 8,631 officers and men were killed, 37,264 were wounded and 40,342 were counted as missing.

1915

The strategic situation at the start of the second year of the war was dominated by the stalemate on the Western Front where, as John Ewing, the war historian of The Royal Scots, points out, the soldiers were having to come to terms with the reality of trench warfare:

The trenches were only taking shape, and once a man

was dumped in them, there he had to remain until he was relieved. With practically no communication trenches in existence, the men were like prisoners, for normally there could be no daylight journeying between the support and front trenches, and a man had little more to do than sit in mud and water, gazing at the sloppy breastworks in front of him. With movement so greatly restricted it is not surprising that men sometimes fell into moods of profound despondency; they had no water except for drinking, they were limited to a diet of bully beef and bread or biscuits, and their chief companions were their own thoughts. Only at night, under showers of bullets and shells, was exercise with any freedom possible. On the conclusion of a spell of trench duty a man resembled a scarecrow, every furrow of his face filled with mud and a stubbly beard on his chin.

Later in the year, conditions would improve and the trench system on both sides of the line became relatively sophisticated and reasonably habitable. They might have been basic, occasionally unsanitary and frequently verminous, but they offered safety to their inhabitants with a complicated system of underground shelters, support and communication trenches protected by breastworks and barbed wire. Between them and the German line lay no man's land, a space of open ground which could be as wide as 300 yards or as narrow as 25 yards. From the air it looked orderly and secure, but the creation of the trench system also dominated the tactics used by both sides and would scarcely change until the return to more open warfare in the last months of the war. In 1915, the dilemma facing British and French planners was how to break the German trench line by attacking key points which would force the enemy to fall back on its lines of communication, and in so doing return some fluidity to the fighting. Lines of advance had to be chosen, and in January the Allies agreed to mount offensives against both sides of the German salient, which ran from Flanders to Verdun. These would be made at Aubers Ridge and Vimy Ridge to the north and in Champagne to the south, the intention being to squeeze the Germans and perhaps even converge to complete the encirclement of the salient. In this spring offensive the British and the French would attack in Flanders and Artois, the French alone in the Champagne. For the British this would involve them in battles at Neuve Chapelle, Aubers Ridge and Festubert and later in the year at Loos. All failed to achieve the Allies' objectives and all produced large numbers of casualties.

By 1915, the Royals had seven battalions in France and Flanders – in addition to the 1st and 2nd battalions, there were two Territorial Force battalions (1/8th and 1/9th) and three New Army battalions (11th, 12th and 13th), all of which took part in the year's battles. In August the 1/8th battalion was given a new role as the pioneer battalion for the 51st (Highland) Division, a Territorial Force formation, and in October the 1st battalion was transferred to the Salonika front in the fighting against Bulgaria. The 2nd battalion served on the Ypres sector throughout the year and took part in the attack on Hooge during the second Battle of Loos in September. Both the 1/8th and 1/9th battalions took part in the second Battle of Ypres in April, when the Germans used poisonous gas for the first time, and both sustained large numbers of casualties. For the regiment's New Army battalions, the major event of the year was their participation in the Battle of Loos in September, when half of the 72 battalions used in the assault phase bore Scottish titles. The 11th and 12th battalions served in 9th (Scottish) Division while the 13th battalion served in 15th (Scottish) Division.

Loos has been called many things by the soldiers who fought in it and also by historians who have picked over its bones, but most are agreed that the best description is that it was both an unnecessary and an unwanted battle. In strategic terms it was meaningless. The attacking divisions gained a salient two miles deep, and in the early stages of the battle some Scottish battalions had the heady sensation of advancing steadily across no man's land, but the end result did little to help a French offensive in Artois and Champagne, the main reason why Kitchener insisted that the battle should take place. At the same time, the Germans had learned the lessons of the Allied attacks earlier in the year and had created second defensive lines on the reverse slopes to compensate for their lack of reserves, and by occupying the higher ground they enjoyed an open field of fire. Both were used to good effect when the Allied offensive opened on 25 September and the high casualty figures tell their own story. Given the number of Scottish regiments involved in the battle, scarcely any part of the country was unaffected. The Royals were no exception, and their losses killed were: 11th battalion, 8 officers and 370 soldiers; 12th battalion, 9 officers and 285 soldiers; 13th battalion, 15 officers and 325 soldiers.

1916

In the aftermath of Loos there was one more casualty, when the Commander-in-Chief of the BEF Sir John French was sacked as a result of his handling of the battle and replaced by General Sir Douglas Haig. Haig's military philosophy and approach to the strategic situation on the Western Front were equally clear-cut. Looking at the trench system which separated the rival armies, he argued that far from being permanent or an insuperable obstacle, it was the key to victory. Once the Allies had built up large enough armies backed by overwhelming firepower, they could attack and destroy the German positions with complete confidence. Successful infantry and artillery assaults would then allow cavalry to exploit the breakthrough by sweeping into open country to turn the German system of defence and ultimately defeat the enemy by removing its ability to resist. It was against that background that Haig contemplated the planning for the major offensive of 1916 – the Battle of the Somme.

The tactics produced by Haig were deceptively simple. He aimed to attack the German lines using the maximum force at his disposal, to break the defences and then to move forward to take possession of the area to the rear. Following an enormous week-long bombardment involving the firing of a million shells along a 25-mile front, the Germans would be in no condition to resist and the British infantry would simply brush the opposition aside as they took possession of the German lines. A creeping barrage would keep the surviving Germans cowering in their trenches. Alas for those fond hopes, the Somme was to be remembered not for the expected breakthrough, but as the killing ground of the British Army – no other battlefield of the First World War created more casualties per square yard and the opening day of the battle, 1 July 1916, was to produce the bloodiest day for the infantry regiments which took part in the initial attack. From the 11 divisions which began the assault, 57,470 men became casualties – 21,392 killed or missing, 35,493 wounded and 585 taken prisoner. It would take another 140 days before the fighting in the sector finally came to an end.

At half past seven on 1 July whistles blew along the front lines as the first wave of British infantrymen went into the attack. As the noise of the explosions died away, men clambered up the scaling ladders and began their advance in the suddenly eerie silence of a summer's morning. Bucked up by the sound and fury of the earlier bombardment, most of the men in the first wave were confident that nothing could have survived such a maelstrom, and while they were naturally nervous and anxious, they believed that they were about to participate in one of the glorious moments of the war. Sergeant Francis Halcrow Scott of the 16th battalion proudly told his parents that 'man to man we could beat them [the Germans] every time'.

Two days later, what was left of the assault battalions was relieved, and withdrew into the rear areas. Amongst them were the two Royal Scots battalions in 34th Division which had taken their objectives south of La Boiselle, despite suffering heavy casualties. The reaction of the survivors in 16th battalion provides another example of the doggedness and courage of the soldiers of the New Army. It had been a dreadful few days, but life had to go on. As a soldier wrote in *The Scotsman* after the war, on 15 December 1919:

> The most wonderful thing of all was that no man seemed to realise that he was doing anything heroic or out of common. Hungry and thirsty, the men had been but there was no grousing. Amid all the scenes of horror and tragedy their sense of humour never failed them. Once two Germans (caught in no-man's-land) came tearing across to our trench, being shot at by their own people in front of us. They dropped into our trench. When one of them, over six feet in height, overcome with thankfulness at finding himself in safety, with blood streaming down a wounded nose, took a dapper officer of ours round the neck, and with a bloody nose attempted to kiss him, the men nearby roared with laughter at the consternation depicted on the British officer's face.

The Somme became known as the graveyard of Kitchener's New Armies, and in no other formations were the losses more grievously felt than in the 'pals' battalions, the units whose soldiers came from the same locality or profession. Ten New Army divisions took part in the battle, and for the more recently arrived soldiers this was their first and, for many, their only experience of combat. Three Scottish divisions were involved at the Somme – 9th and 15th Scottish Divisions and the 51st (Highland) Division – but there were Scottish battalions serving in other divisions. The Royals had three battalions serving in the 34th (15th and 16th) and 35th Divisions (17th). As happened in the rest of the country whole areas were affected when the casualty lists began to appear and the Royals were no exception. Both Cranston's and McCrae's battalions took part in the initial assault with 34th Division, which attacked the heavily fortified German position at La Boiselle and suffered accordingly. The 15th lost 18 officers and 610 soldiers killed, wounded or missing, while the casualties in the 16th were 12 officers and 573 soldiers. In addition to the 2nd battalion and 1/9th battalion, the Royals' other New Army battalions on the Somme were the 11th, 12th and 13th.

By the time the fighting on the Somme came to an end in November, the Allies had lost 600,000 casualties, two thirds of them British, while the German losses cannot have been much less. However, it was not all in vain. Although the expected breakthrough never occurred, and the ground gained was a modest return for the expenditure of so many lives and so much *matériel*, pressure had been taken off the French and valuable lessons had been learned. After the war, senior German commanders complained that the Somme was 'the muddy grave of the German field army', while their opposite numbers in the British Army argued that their inexperienced divisions came of age during the battle, even though most of the lessons were bloodily learned.

Sir John Hepburn, the founder of The Royal Scots, who served as the first colonel of the regiment between 1633 and 1636. The portrait has been attributed to Daniel Mytens, who worked during the same period. (Courtesy of The Royal Scots Regimental Museum)

Colonel Sir Robert Douglas recovers the Regiment's Colour during the Battle of Steenkirke, 3 August 1692.
(Courtesy of The Royal Scots Regimental Museum)

The 2ⁿᵈ battalion on the march in 1688, two years after its
formation. The painting is also known as 'the horse's bum'.
Watercolour by Granville Baker, 1939.
(Courtesy of The Royal Scots Regimental Museum)

The 3ʳᵈ battalion took part in Wellington's operations in the Peninsula and
were present at the Battle of Corunna on 16 January 1809, when they helped
to repulse Marshal Soult's main attack. Watercolour by D. Dighton, 1812.
(Courtesy of The Royal Scots Regimental Museum)

Group of officers of the 2nd battalion at Shahjehanpur in India in 1871.
Note the mixture of civilian dress and military uniforms.
(Courtesy of The Royal Scots Regimental Museum)

The 2nd battalion marches past Lieutenant-General Sir Horace Smith–Dorrien
(mounted, left) in Plymouth, 1913. Within a year, they would be fighting in France
as part of British II Corps. (Courtesy of The Royal Scots Regimental Museum)

Men of the 9th (Highlanders) battalion on the road from Amiens to Albert in September 1916. The 'Dandy Ninth' was the only Royal Scots battalion to wear the kilt. (© Imperial War Museum)

Riflemen of the 5th battalion cleaning their weapons while out of the line at Suvla in Gallipoli. Three Royal Scots battalions served in this ill-fated operation and suffered high casualties. (© Imperial War Museum)

The 7th battalion on a route march while acclimatising in Egypt in 1916. After serving in Gallipoli, the battalions of The Royal Scots took part in the next campaign against Turkish forces, in Palestine.
(Courtesy of The Royal Scots Regimental Museum)

Over 800 British prisoners of war, many of them Royal Scots, were drowned when the freighter *Lisbon Maru* was torpedoed in the China Sea in October 1942. Pencil sketch of the final moments by Lieutenant W.C. Johnston, US Navy. (Courtesy of The Royal Scots Regimental Museum)

By the end of the Second World War, British infantrymen had the use of tracked vehicles to transport them. A section of the 8th battalion mounted on a Kangaroo, which was basically a Sherman tank with the gun turret removed. (Courtesy of The Royal Scots Regimental Museum)

The 7/9th battalion served in 52nd (Lowland) Division, which was trained for mountain warfare. They are being inspected by the Colonel-in-Chief, HRH The Princess Royal, in August 1942. (© Imperial War Museum)

Dedication of the 1st battalion memorial to those Royal Scots who died in the Battle of Kohima and the opening of the Imphal Road. It was dedicated on 25 November 1944, with the service being taken by the Reverend Crichton Robertson. (Courtesy of The Royal Scots Regimental Museum)

Following their participation in the Suez campaign of 1956, the 1st battalion returned to Scotland. They were presented with new colours in the grounds of Holyrood Palace by the Colonel-in-Chief on 4 October 1957. (Courtesy of The Royal Scots Regimental Museum)

Between May 1964 and February 1965, the 1st battalion served in Aden and the Radfan on internal security duties. A picket of A Company, with Sergeant Dickie on the right and Corporal Ward on the left.
(Courtesy of The Royal Scots Regimental Museum)

In the 1970s and 1980s, at the height of the Troubles, the 1st battalion were regularly deployed in Northern Ireland. A patrol of B Company receives orders on a street in Belfast. (Courtesy of The Royal Scots Regimental Museum)

In 1990–91, the 1st battalion took part in the operations to oust Iraqi forces from Kuwait. Lieutenant-Colonel Iain Johnston (standing in the foreground) gives his orders after the taking of objective BRASS on 26 February 1991.
(Courtesy of The Royal Scots Regimental Museum)

1917

The first major offensive of the year was the Battle of Arras, which began after the German high command decided to shorten the line between Arras and the Aisne by constructing new and heavily fortified defences which would be their new 'final' position behind the Somme battlefield. Known to the Germans as the *Siegfried Stellung* and to the Allies as the Hindenburg Line, this formidable construction shortened the front by some 30 miles and created an obstacle which would not be taken until the end of the war. The withdrawal began on 16 March, and as the Germans retired they laid waste to the countryside, leaving a devastated landscape in which the cautiously pursuing Allies had to build new trench systems. To test the reality of the withdrawal and to ascertain the potency of the new German positions, raids were ordered on the enemy trenches and inevitably these caused high casualties. They were also dreaded by the men who took part in them: in one such raid on 21 March the 11th battalion sustained 75 casualties. Raids took place at night and usually involved up to three sections consisting of eight men each, who had to cross no man's land armed with grenades. According to one soldier, 'the object of the raid was to kill Germans, damage his trenches and obtain his identification'.

The overall direction of the British and Canadian forces was under the command of General Sir Edmund Allenby, a thrusting cavalryman who was known as 'The Bull'. While four Canadian divisions attacked the Vimy Ridge, ten divisions made their assault on a broad front, twelve miles wide, straddling the valley of the River Scarpe to the east of Arras. The battle began in the early morning of 9 April in a biting wind which sent snow flurries scudding across the countryside, but despite the wintry weather the portents were good. For the first time, the assault battalions found that the artillery had done its job by destroying the wire, and new types of gas shells had fallen in the rear areas, killing

German transport horses and making the movement of guns impossible. The first phase of the battle encouraged hopes that this might be the long-awaited breakthrough and some units were surprised both by the ease of their attack and the lack of German resistance. For example, all eight Royal Scots' battalions achieved their first-day objectives and moved forward so quickly that they found themselves coming under friendly fire from their own guns. It was at this point that things began to fall apart.

Despite the initial successes the British advance had been irregular and some units were held up by German defensive positions which had escaped the barrage and were still able to inflict heavy casualties on the attacking forces. In the assault on the Blue Line near Bois de la Maison, the 15th battalion was reduced to four officers with around a hundred men and, according to the regimental historian, 'once again raw courage was called for before the enemy could be silenced and officers and men immediately rose to the challenge'. Attacking with them were the men of the 16th battalion, who lost two officers during an attack on a particularly tenacious German machine-gun position. Their day ended, as it did for all the attacking battalions, with ground gained and the possibility of taking more. As night fell the weather deteriorated, leaving the infantrymen in forward positions exposed, hungry and bitterly cold, as they had been forbidden to wear or carry their greatcoats during the attack.

Despite those problems, Allenby ordered the attack to be resumed the following day with an assault on the final German line at Monchy. He was optimistic of success, but already the Germans had started moving their reserves from their pre-battle positions 15 miles behind the lines. At headquarters, Haig ordered further attacks and, spurred on by his commander-in-chief, Allenby urged his men to press on with the next phase of the battle. Monchy fell on 12 April, but time was fast running out for the ever more

THE FIRST WORLD WAR: THE WESTERN FRONT

exhausted assault battalions. Increased German resistance and reinforcement meant higher casualties for the attackers. The 11th battalion lost 150 casualties and the 12th battalion 250 in the course of an attempt to take the village of Roeux, with its chemical works, north of the Scarpe between Fampoux and Plouvain. On 15 April, almost a week after the first attack, Haig succumbed to reason and to the pleas of three divisional commanders and called a halt to the first phase of the battle to allow reinforcements to be brought up.

In the next phase of the battle there were to be no easy gains, and the British attack soon faltered as the assault battalions came up against stronger German opposition, and Allenby was forced to scale down the offensive. Some of the fiercest fighting was at Rouex, which had been captured briefly only for it to be retaken by the Germans. On 28 April, a fresh assault on the village was made by 34th Division and, in common with other operations at this stage of the battle, it was hurried and improvised. The preceding artillery barrage failed to unsettle the German defenders, who were in the process of rushing reinforcements into the village for an attack of their own. In the confusion, forward elements of 16th battalion found themselves cut off, having reached their objective ahead of the other attacking battalions, and as a result they sustained heavy losses.

By the time the fighting ended at the beginning of May, any hope of defeating the Germans at Arras had disappeared and the losses had multiplied. The British suffered around 159,000 casualties, a daily rate of 4,076 (higher than the Somme's 2,943), and the stuffing had been knocked out of many of the formations, which had been involved in a month of hard fighting against a heavily reinforced enemy. Later in the year, at the Third Battle of Ypres, also known as Passchendaele, all three Scottish divisions were again involved in the fighting to deepen the British-held

Ypres Salient. The battle lasted four months and accounted for a quarter of a million casualties, 70,000 of them killed or drowned in the lagoons of mud which covered the battlefield. During the fighting the 16th battalion was reduced to 4 officers and 130 soldiers and the 11th and 12th battalions lost so many casualties that for a time they were incapable of taking further offensive action.

1918

In an all-or-nothing attempt to regain the initiative to win the war before US forces entered the struggle, the Germans planned a major offensive for March. This would drive a wedge between the two opposing armies, striking through the old Somme battlefield between Arras and La Fère before turning to destroy the British Third and Fifth Armies on the left of the Allied line. Codenamed 'Michael', it called for a massive rolling 'hurricane' artillery barrage followed by a rapid and aggressive advance by the infantry which would punch a hole in the British defences and lay the foundations for defeating the enemy in Flanders. Strong-points would be bypassed to be wrapped up later by the mopping-up troops. The fighting began in the early hours of the morning of 21 March, when the German artillery produced a huge bombardment which lasted for five hours and which left the defenders badly shaken and disorientated. Gas and smoke shells added to the confusion, which was increased by an early morning mist, leaving commanders with no exact idea of where and when the infantry attack was coming. On the Arras sector, held by XVII Corps, the brunt of the German attack fell on the 15th Scottish Division south of the Scarpe and the divisional commander was told by his superiors in no uncertain terms that there was to be no withdrawal and no surrender. Heavily involved in the fighting were eight battalions of The Royal Scots, five with the Third Army (2nd, 1/8th, 13th, 15th, 16th) and three (1/9th, 11th, 12th) with the Fifth Army. One company of the 1/9th battalion suffered huge casualties while covering the withdrawal of the 20th Division at Le Quesnoy – out of 100 men there were only 11 survivors. Later, two further Royal Scots battalions, 5/6th and 17th, were rushed into action as reinforcements.

A week later, the Germans called off the attack. Casualties on both sides were high: the British lost 76,000, the French 35,000 and on the German side there were 109,000 casualties. During the withdrawal to Bailleul in the third week of April the 15th and 16th battalions were combined and a month later, on 16 May, both battalions were disbanded when the 34th Division was suspended as a result of the losses in battle and the lack of reinforcements. By then only some 30 of McCrae's original volunteers were left in the battalion, and they and the remainder of the battalion were posted to other Royal Scots battalions. During the summer the 8th, 9th and 13th battalions took part in the fighting in support of the French army on the Marne and all Royal Scots battalions serving in France, including the 4th and 7th battalions (recently arrived from Palestine), were involved in the final 'hundred days' offensive in the late summer which defeated the Germans on the Western Front.

SEVEN

THE FIRST WORLD WAR: GALLIPOLI, PALESTINE, SALONIKA AND RUSSIA

The Western Front was not the only area of operations in which The Royal Scots were involved. Although the trench systems and the great battles of attrition on the Western Front have come to represent all that was unlovely about the First World War, the British Army also fought on a number of other battle fronts. The war took place on a global scale, and Scottish soldiers fought on all of its main battle fronts – Gallipoli, Mesopotamia, Palestine, Salonika and Italy. Of these, the bloodiest and most costly in terms of casualties were the first three, which involved fighting against the armies of the Ottoman Empire. (Turkey had joined forces with the Germans in the early days of the war.) The Royals were not involved in Mesopotamia, but their battalions fought in Gallipoli and Palestine and also took part in the operations against Bulgarian forces on the Salonika front. The final deployment is almost a historical curiosity: once the war had come to an end, the 2/10th battalion, a Territorial Force formation, was still taking part in an ill-fated intervention to support non-Communist forces in Russia in the civil war of 1919.

The operations against Ottoman forces in Gallipoli, Mesopotamia and Palestine were part of a wider initiative to break the impasse of the Western Front by opening new fronts elsewhere. As it became clear that the war of movement had ended on the Western Front by the end of 1914, so began the debate between the 'westerners' and the 'easterners'. The former argued that Germany could only be defeated convincingly in Europe while the 'easterners' believed that the impasse could be broken by using the ships of the French navy and the Royal Navy to attack the Turkish positions in Gallipoli and knock Turkey out of the war. Then ground forces would be landed to complete the capture of the peninsula and neutralise the Turkish garrison. The naval plan was put into operation on 19 February 1915, but it soon ran into trouble. Not only did the battleships fail to make much impression on the Turkish defences, but it had proved impossible to sweep minefields, due to the accuracy of the Turkish field guns and the strength of the local currents. Several major British and French ships were sunk or damaged, and the decision was taken to land forces on the peninsula in an ill-conceived amphibious operation under the overall command of Lieutenant-General Sir Ian Hamilton. At the beginning of March it was agreed to earmark the British 29th Division to support landings by light infantry battalions of the Royal Naval Division. Kitchener then ordered the deployment of Australian and New Zealand troops training in Egypt, while the French agreed to deploy the *Corps Expéditionnaire d'Orient*, a mixed force of French and North African troops.

The attack was planned to begin on 25 April, six weeks after the naval bombardment had spluttered to a halt. The main offensive was aimed at the Cape Helles beaches, and was directed by Major-

General Aylmer Hunter-Weston, a Royal Engineer who had been born at Hunterston in Ayrshire in 1864. Known throughout the army as 'Hunter-Bunter' he was a hard and aggressive commander who frequently declared that he cared nothing about casualties provided that results were achieved; with his gruff red-faced ferocity he might have been a figure of fun had he not been in such an important position. His 29th Division ('The Incomparable') was considered to be one of the best-trained in the army, and it contained the first of The Royal Scots to take part in the Gallipoli theatre – 1/5th battalion which had been mobilised in Edinburgh in August 1914, and had been employed on coastal defence duties before joining Hunter-Weston's division in March 1915. But before they could give an account of themselves in the fighting they had to be taken ashore. That proved to be no easy task. In addition to a specially adapted Clyde-built collier, the *River Clyde*, which was run ashore at V beach carrying 2,000 men, the main force was landed in ships' cutters pulled by a variety of tug boats. The intention was to secure the beaches and then to advance on the ridge between Krithia and Achi Baba which would be the key to taking control of the peninsula. As was the case throughout the campaign things did not turn out that way.

In the initial stages, the Turks seemed confused by the breadth and strength of the Allied attack, but they soon regrouped and at V and W beaches the British forces took heavy casualties when they found themselves pinned down by heavy and accurate machine-gun fire. On the other hand, the landings at X and Y beaches were unopposed, but there were serious communication failures between the two landing forces which meant that they were unable to exploit the situation even though they faced minimal Turkish opposition. Forced to dig in quickly, the attacking forces used their packs to reinforce their defences, and later admitted that the 'trenches' never deserved the name. By the next day, both sides had taken large numbers of casualties; the British alone had lost 700 killed or wounded. Although the 1/5th battalion was held in reserve during the initial landings, it was quickly brought up in support and one of the Royals taking part in the landings, Bandsman G.G. McKay, revealed in a letter home the difficulties facing the soldiers as they attempted to get ashore under enemy fire:

> We have to be prepared to land waist–deep in water. Carry haversack on top of pack, two days' rations, bayonet in pack also, spare bandolier of ammunition, 250 rounds issued to all. Emergency ration – biscuits, two oxo cubes, tea, sugar and bully beef in tins.

With Hunter-Weston unable or unwilling to comprehend the seriousness of the position and the need for immediate reinforcement, a decision was taken to retire to the beaches for re-embarkation. The failure to act decisively at Y beach was compounded by Hamilton's unwillingness to intervene in Hunter-Weston's direction of the battle and, according to the Official Historian, those blunders typified the operation with its confusion over command, the lack of initiative after landing and the absence of any support from the staff:

> Cleverly conceived, happily opened, hesitatingly concluded, miserably ended – such is the story of the landing at Y beach. In deciding to throw a force ashore at that point, Sir Ian Hamilton would seem to have hit upon the key of the whole situation. Favoured by an unopposed landing, and by the absence of any Turks in the neighbourhood for many hours, it is as certain as anything can be in war that a bold advance from Y beach

on the morning of 25th April must have freed the southern beaches that morning, and ensured a decisive victory for the 29th Division. But apart from its original conception, no other part of the operation was free from calamitous mistakes, and Fortune seldom smiles on a force that neglects its own opportunities.

Even at that early stage, stalemate had come to the battlefield. The Allies were confined to their beach-head, while the Turks held onto the higher ground and could not be dislodged, largely due to the doggedness of their opposition and the lack of field artillery. At the same time, the Turks failed to drive their enemy back into the sea and the fighting degenerated into as bitter a struggle as anything seen on the Western Front. By the end of the month, less than a week after they had landed, the British had lost some 400 officers and 8,500 soldiers, around one-third of the attacking force. The 1/5th battalion had lost heavily in their first attack after the landings, with three officers killed and the commanding officer and his second-in-command badly wounded. It was immediately clear to Hamilton that he needed more troops. At the beginning of May the first reinforcements arrived, in the shape of the 29th Indian Infantry Brigade and the 42nd (East Lancashire) Division, but it was clear that a much bigger force was needed to dislodge the Turkish defenders. On 10 May, Kitchener sanctioned the dispatch of the 52nd (Lowland) Division, a Territorial formation which included 1/4th Royal Scots and 1/7th Royal Scots. (One other Royal Scots battalion served in Gallipoli – the 1st Garrison Battalion – which had been formed in Edinburgh in August 1914 and was composed of older men or those unfit for active service.) The 52nd (Lowland) Division began deploying immediately, with the battalions being sent south by train from their training area near Stirling to

Liverpool and Devonport for passage to Gallipoli. It was a well-oiled operation, but tragedy hit one of The Royal Scots battalions even before it had reached the seat of war.

Half of the Leith-based 1/7th Royal Scots was travelling south from Larbert on Train 18 when it slammed into a local service at Quintinshill Junction near Gretna at 6.45 a.m. on 22 May as a result of a disastrous misunderstanding by the signalmen, who had put the local service on the same track as The Royal Scots' train. The carriages of both trains were strewn across the main line, but as the survivors struggled to come to terms with their predicament, worse was to follow. Within minutes, the disaster was compounded when a London to Glasgow overnight express travelling north at high speed crashed into the wreckage, causing even greater damage. Then, to the horror of the rescuers, 'a few wisps of smoke were seen to start in different parts of the mass, and soon the wreckage was blazing furiously – and there were no available means of coping with the fire'. Because the carriages were constructed of wood and contained gas cylinders for the internal lighting, a huge conflagration was inevitable.

In the aftermath of the disaster it was found that 3 officers and 207 soldiers had been killed; 5 officers and 219 soldiers had been injured and the battalion was forced to travel out to Gallipoli at half strength. When the funerals were held in Leith's Rosebank Cemetery, Edinburgh's port area was in mourning with blinds drawn, shops closed and huge crowds lining the route of the mass funeral procession. Both the signalmen involved in the accident, James Tinsley and George Meakin, were tried at the High Court in Edinburgh and found guilty of negligence: Meakin was imprisoned for eighteen months while Tinsley received three years but suffered a nervous breakdown while in prison. At the time it was the biggest disaster in Britain's railway history, and it was a terrible blow for a city which would soon be mourning even greater numbers of dead from Gallipoli and from the autumn battles in Flanders.

During the 52nd (Lowland) Division's first major offensive at Helles on 28 June, the assault battalions included the 1/4th and the 1/7th; they both suffered terribly from the intensive Turkish machine-gun fire and the failure of the British artillery to suppress it. The Royals lost heavily: the 1/4th battalion had 16 officers and 204 soldiers killed or missing, while the 1/7th battalion had been reduced to 6 officers and 169 soldiers, roughly the size of a company. As lists started appearing in the Edinburgh newspapers citing The Royal Scots' casualties, it was impossible to disguise the fact that whole areas of the city had been affected and that, as the *Evening Dispatch* reflected, death had been unsparing of class or background:

> In its ranks are many former pupils of such schools as George Watson's College, not a few of whom joined after the outbreak of the war. There is something at once inspiring and pathetic in the fate of these young fellows. They had grown up together almost from infancy, sitting on the same bench at school, romping in the playground together, running shoulder to shoulder on the football field, and then after the parting that comes at the end of school life, finding themselves side by side once more on the field of battle, playing the biggest game that men have ever played.

The sentiment comes close to delineating the ethos of the volunteer army, its tight solidarity and its optimism in the face of hardship and violent death. And those losses were made more poignant because they mirrored not just Edinburgh's social structure but also the close-knit composition of the territorial battalions, in which many professional men served as private soldiers either because there were not enough commissions or because they wanted to stay with their friends. Listed in the daily and ever-growing catalogue of death was Captain George McCrae, 1/4th Royal Scots, the elder son of the founder of the 16th Royal Scots. All across the central belt of the Scottish Lowlands, families were left to mourn the loss of young lives as the casualties began to mount in the battalions of their local regiments. In an attempt to humanise the process, the local newspapers printed brief details about each casualty and, wherever possible, a photograph of the young man in uniform. What the writers could not do was to describe the dreadful conditions being faced by the men. Not only was the fighting conducted at close quarters, with some trenches being almost in touching distance, but the physical hardships were worse than anything faced on the Western Front. Despite the best efforts at maintaining basic sanitation, disease was rampant, especially dysentery and enteric fever, which was spread by the absence of proper latrines and washing facilities and by the ever-present swarms of black buzzing flies. In the heat of high summer the swarms were especially bad, and even the advent of colder autumn weather brought little respite as the sun gave way to long days of freezing rain.

Despite the arrival of reinforcements – in all, Hamilton was given five new divisions – the deadlock could not be broken and the men on the peninsula were becoming increasingly weakened. An ambitious amphibious landing at Suvla Bay failed in August because the Turks were able to rush reinforcements into the area to prevent the creation of a bridgehead. In October the inevitable happened: Hamilton was sacked, rightly so as his leadership had become increasingly feeble and sterile, and he was replaced by General Sir Charles Monro, a veteran of the fighting on the Western Front who was also a disciple of the westerners. Having taken stock of the situation he recommended evacuation, although this was not accepted until the beginning of November, when Kitchener himself visited the battle front and found himself agreeing that the difficulties were insuperable. A heavy and unexpected winter storm also helped to decide the issue – over 280 British soldiers died of exposure, including a number from The Worcestershire Regiment who were found frozen to death on the fire steps of their trenches. In a brilliant operation, which was all the more inspired after the fiascos which had preceded it, the British finally withdrew their forces at the end of 1915, remarkably without losing any casualties. The great adventure to win the war by other means was finally over, but many of the survivors, including Lance-Corporal Louden of the 1/4th battalion, had mixed emotions when they said farewell to one of the harshest battlefields of the war. His diary is held by the Imperial War Museum:

> By 3.30 a.m. on the 9th of January, 1916, the evacuation of our forces from Gallipoli had been completed without the loss of a single man. Time-fuses to magazines, dumps, etc, had been lit, and in a short time abandoned tents and heaps of stores and supplies burst into flames. At 4 a.m. the two magazines under Cape Helles were blown up. At last the Turks realised that something unusual was happening.
>
> So, amidst a final blaze of mighty pyres and bursting shells that lit up the black clouds scurrying overhead, amidst detonations that reverberated among and seemed to shake the surrounding isles and mountains, and amidst the storm and fury of the wind and sea, the Gallipoli campaign came to an end.

One statistic will stand for many: when the 1/4th battalion was evacuated, it had been reduced to 2 officers and 148 men. As on other fronts during the war, the exact British death toll was difficult to compute, but most experts agree that 36,000 deaths from combat and disease is not an unrealistic tally. The official British statistics show 117,549 casualties – 28,200 killed, 78,095 wounded, 11,254 missing. Total Allied casualties were put at 265,000.

The failure of the Gallipoli campaign has provided history with one of its great conundrums, the conditional 'if only' being applied to most aspects of it. If only the tactics, the leadership, the reinforcements and the munitions had been better; if only the execution had matched the conception, then a sordid defeat could have been a glittering triumph. The original reasons for the deployment had much to recommend them, but an absence of clear thinking and the half-hearted conduct of the campaign must account for its failure and for the waste of so many lives and so much equipment. With conditions worse than anything witnessed on the Western Front and a more concentrated rate of attrition, Gallipoli was a long nightmare. Some soldiers, like William Begbie, A Company, 1/7th Royal Scots, looked back with pride and some amusement when he thought of his 16-year-old self attacking the Turkish lines, but at the same time he also recorded that the fighting was brutal and deadly, with the enemy producing 'such a terrific fire that our Company fell in bundles':

> The enemy artillery bombarded our trenches from 9 a.m. till 11 a.m. They scored many direct hits on our lines. We suffered many casualties before we even left our trenches. At last the hour came and at the words 'Over you go lads', the troops gave vent to one resounding cheer and swarmed over the parapets into the perils of the open ground. On

the signal to charge, I caught hold of a root and started to pull myself up but near the top the root came away in my hand and I fell back into the trench. Before the 'Charge' order came, when I was lying in the bottom of the trench with the noise of the shells bursting and the machine-guns firing, the only place I did not want to go was over the parapet, but when I fell back the only place I didn't want to be was in the trench when the rest of the Company were shouting and charging over the top. I ran up the trench so it was easier to climb over the parapet. When I got to my feet I remembered our instructions, so I kept yelling, rifle at the ready and ran like hell into the enemy trenches. Before I reached it I could see some Turks retreating to their next lines.

In addition to producing a vividly written diary (held by the Imperial War Museum), William Begbie has one other claim to fame: in common with many other soldiers who volunteered to serve in the First World War he was under-age and had lied about his date of birth when he enlisted in the 1/7th battalion in August 1914. He was in fact only 15. However, it was not the end of the war for him and the other survivors. Most of the forces were sent back to France in time to take part in the Battle of the Somme while others, including the 52nd (Lowland) Division, were sent to Egypt to guard the Suez Canal and to train for the forthcoming operations against Ottoman forces in Palestine and Syria.

PALESTINE

The next great prize was the defeat of the Turkish forces in Palestine, and the operation was entrusted to an Egyptian expeditionary force of 88,000 soldiers, under the command of General Sir Edmund Allenby, who had been warned by the Prime Minister,

David Lloyd George, that he had to take Jerusalem by Christmas as a gift to the British nation. There were other imperatives. With no sign of a breakthrough on the Western Front, Lloyd George hoped that the defeat of Turkey would be a major blow to the Germans and perhaps hasten the end of the war without further costly offensives in France and Flanders. From the outset Allenby recognised that he needed overwhelming superiority over the Turks if he were to avoid the setbacks at Gallipoli, but getting the reinforcements in the second half of 1917 was another matter. The priority continued to be the Western Front, and with the Battle of Passchendaele (or Third Ypres) eating up resources, it took time and much subtle diplomacy to build up his forces. Amongst them was the 52nd (Lowland) Division with its two Royal Scots battalions. Their objective was to break into Palestine through Gaza and Beersheba and destroy the defending Turkish Eighth Army.

Allenby's battle-plan was innovatory, yet simple, and was based largely on his reading of the terrain over which the fighting would take place. On 27 October, following a huge bombardment from artillery and from British and French warships lying off the coast, Gaza was attacked while XXI Corps prepared for the break-in battle which would follow. At the same time, and in great secrecy, Allenby shifted the emphasis of his attack towards Beersheba, which was quickly surrounded by a brilliant flanking attack to the east. Not only had the objective been taken, but Beersheba's vital water supplies had been captured and the Turks were powerless to bring up reserves. The fall of Beersheba allowed Allenby's forces to put greater pressure on the Turkish positions at Gaza, and its defences were successfully stormed on 7 November, leaving the defenders no option but to retreat north up the littoral towards Askalon and Jaffa. During this mobile phase of the battle the Turks fought with great determination, but they were demoralised by the weight of the attack and by the use of British warplanes to strafe their fleeing columns. A diary kept by Major W.R. Kermack who commanded a company in the 1/7th battalion, gives a vivid impression of the kind of fighting in which the Royals were involved against Turkish forces during the capture of Gaza:

> The Turkish artillery opened up on us almost at once with shrapnel and high explosive; but we pushed right on, almost without checking, across the Wady al Mejma, which proved to be 12 to 15 feet deep, with steep but broken sides. Then, coming under machine-gun fire, both from the ridge for which we were making and from the flanks, we ran forward to the second Wady (which was, I think, the enemy's first trench). This was much shallower, indeed, hardly breast-high, and there we formed a firing line. Our line seemed very thin, but the longer we stayed in this trench the more accurate the enemy shrapnel became. The only course was to push on; and the line worked up, bit by bit, quite on the Drill Book pattern, coming at last under the curve of the crest, to find the shallow trench there by that time almost unoccupied.

The fall of Gaza opened the way to Jerusalem and, to great acclaim, the holy city fell on 8 December after a determined attack. Three days later, in a carefully stage-managed operation, Allenby and his staff entered the city to take possession of it and to secure the holy places. To avoid hurting Islamic feelings, the Mosque of Omar was put under the protection of Indian Muslim troops, and the guards lining the streets came from the four home countries, Australia and New Zealand, and France and Italy. It was not the end of the war in Palestine, but it was the beginning of the end. Allenby's next objectives were to move into Judea and to regroup to prevent Turkish counter-attacks before moving on to his next objectives: Beirut, Damascus and Aleppo. However, to accomplish that he would need additional troops to reinforce his own men and to protect the lines of communication as he pushed north; at the very least, he told the War Office, he would need an additional 16 divisions, including one of cavalry. In the short term, his forces invested Jaffa, which fell after the 52nd (Lowland) Division seized the banks of the River Auja in an operation which demanded surprise and resulted in 'the most furious hand-to-hand encounters of the campaign'. This proved to be the last action undertaken by the Royals in Palestine. Before the question of reinforcing Allenby could be addressed, the Allies were faced by a crisis on the Western Front in March 1918, and the need for rapid reinforcement meant that the 52nd (Lowland) Division had to return to France.

SALONIKA

The withdrawal from Gallipoli allowed the British and the French to build up forces in the Balkans, both to support Serbia and to prevent Bulgarian forces from influencing events in the region – on 5 October 1915 its army had been mobilised and it entered the war on the side of the Central Powers. The Allied response was to send two divisions to the port of Salonika (Thessaloniki) under the command of the French general, Maurice Sarrail. At the time, German and Austro-Hungarian forces had invaded Serbia and entered Belgrade while Bulgarian forces had pushed into Macedonia, a move which stymied any Allied attempt to relieve pressure on the Serbs. As a result, Sarrail's divisions were pushed back into Salonika, which rapidly became a huge military base – by the end of the year three French and five British divisions, together with a huge amount of stores and ammunition, were encamped in a perimeter which was 200 miles square and defended by acres of barbed wire. For entirely political reasons, the British supported the deployment, which the Germans ridiculed as 'the greatest internment camp in the world' and which prevented vital reinforcements and equipment from being deployed on the Western Front.

Amongst the 11 Scottish infantry regiments which took part in the campaign was 1st Royal Scots, but it did not see action until the summer of 1916, when British XVI Corps moved up the valley of the River Struma towards the border with Bulgaria. The move was made to encourage Romania to join the war on the Allied side, and most of the fighting was undertaken by the French divisions, which had to face determined Bulgarian counter-attacks. Most of the British effort was confined to the Struma valley, where the participants found that the style of fighting seemed to come from a different age. On 30 September, three Scottish regiments – 1st Royal Scots, 2nd Camerons and 1st Argyll and Sutherland Highlanders – moved across the Struma to attack Bulgarian positions in the fortified villages of Karajakoi Bala and Karajakoi Zir with the Royals' pipers leading them into battle. According to the battalion's *War Diary* 'the pipers marched with the first line and played throughout the charge', but unfortunately the pipe-major was soon wounded and 'looked a sorry sight'. After being given a cigarette by a watching staff officer from 81st Brigade he was taken by stretcher-bearers to a rear area and later recovered from his wounds. For Lieutenant R.W.F. Johnstone of the 1st battalion, who left a vivid description of the fighting, it was not the only arcane touch of the day. The fighting in Salonika was unlike anything seen on the Western Front and was more like a campaign from an earlier age:

> Behind us we could see on the heights spectators watching the battle. On our level we could see the artillery galloping

into action, the guns being swung into position and the teams galloping back to a position of safety while the guns opened fire and the noise of the shells above our heads was at times quite deafening. There was also a cable wagon in front of the gun line galloping across the front with mounted linesmen paying out the cable as they rode. It was in all a scene of the old South African-type battlefield which no one who was there would ever forget.

Both objectives were captured, with the loss of 1,248 casualties, and it was the biggest operation undertaken by British forces in Salonika in 1916. However, it was quickly becoming apparent that the main British losses were not battlefield casualties but men who fell victim to malaria – for every casualty from enemy action, ten found themselves in hospital as a result of illness, and some units were unable to function. Dysentery and various enteric diseases also caused havoc and put a great strain on the medical services, but malaria was a constant problem, mainly because it was endemic in the area and proved difficult to eradicate. Re-infection was also a problem, for although malaria did not kill men in great numbers – fatalities were confined to 1 per cent of hospital admissions – it did remove soldiers from operational service, and in the worst cases incapacitated men had to be evacuated.

The last major actions in Salonika took place in May 1917, with an operation by the French and Serb forces to break through the Bulgarian defensive lines. The British objective, undertaken by XII Corps, was the heavily defended positions to the west of Lake Doiran, but the Allied offensive failed and had to be abandoned on 23 May, with the loss of 5,024 British casualties. As on the Western Front, the Allied artillery failed to cut the wire, and the attacking infantry soon found themselves pinned down by accurate Bulgarian artillery and machine-gun fire. However, the enemy also proved to be surprisingly inefficient, with dilapidated trenches and straggling barbed-wire emplacements which seemed to have been thrown into position without any care. In some places around the village of Homondos, in the Struma valley, which was attacked on 12–13 October, the defences were much less formidable than had been anticipated, as an after-action report by 1st Royal Scots testified:

> The wire looks formidable from a distance [wrote Major Mackenzie, in the brigade *War Diary*], but was very poorly put up. The stakes were short, weak and not properly pointed, and only driven a few inches into the ground. The wire was only twisted loosely round the stakes, and the entanglement was neither high enough nor broad enough. It appeared to me that resolute infantry could have walked over, beaten down or dragged away this wire and that cutting it would have been a mere waste of time.

The mountainous terrain also helped the defenders, and the Commander-in-Chief of British Salonika Forces, Lieutenant-General G.F. Milne, was forced to concede that 'our men are not a match for the Bulgar in hill fighting, though superior on the flat'. (Other problems came from manpower shortages, lack of reliable equipment, especially heavy artillery, and the absence of coherent plans.) For the rest of the year the front remained surprisingly quiet, while XVI Corps' activities in the Struma valley were confined to a series of limited operations which were often little more than skirmishes with an increasingly reluctant enemy.

During the winter, Greece finally entered the war on the Allied side, following the abdication of the pro-German King Constantine, and at last the Allies were rewarded for their long-standing military presence in Salonika. At the same time, Sarrail was sacked and replaced first by General M.L.A. Guillaumat and then by General Franchet D'Esperey, who brought the campaign to a conclusion in the summer of 1918. Weakened by German troop withdrawals, the Bulgarian army failed to halt the last assault of the war, which began on 15 September and ended a fortnight later, when the Bulgarian front was split. On 29 September, French forces entered Skopje, and the following day Bulgaria requested an armistice. D'Esperey was keen to continue his advance up through the Balkans to threaten Germany's southern flank, and his troops were already crossing the Danube when the war came to an end on 11 November. At the same time Milne moved his British forces up to the Turkish frontier, but his hopes of attacking Turkey ended when the Turks signed an armistice on 31 October. Elements of British forces remained in the area into 1919, serving as peacekeepers, and for most of them it was a dispiriting end to a campaign which had tied up huge numbers of men and matériel for no obvious strategic gains. Although the British Salonika Force listed a modest 18,000 casualties from combat, this was overshadowed by the 481,000 who had succumbed to illness, mainly malaria. To put those figures into a regimental perspective, the 1st battalion lost 3 officers and 17 soldiers killed in action and 4 officers and 100 soldiers wounded, but the casualties to illness were much higher. For all concerned it had been a lengthy and ultimately pointless deployment, not least for The Royal Scots. As Colonel Paterson notes in his history, 'for the 1st battalion it had been a disappointing campaign' and 'there was no great rejoicing when hostilities stopped'.

RUSSIA

By the end of 1918 the killing had come to an end on the war's main battle fronts, but in many other parts of the globe the dying went on. In northern Russia, on the banks of the River Dvina, the 2/10th Royal Scots spent Armistice Day repelling an attack by Bolshevik forces which left 19 Scottish soldiers dead and 4 injured. One soldier, Private John Stewart, endured the horrible experience of being wounded in the chest and then witnessing the death by sniper fire of one of his comrades who had tried to help him by applying a field dressing. As darkness fell, Stewart feared that he might freeze to death, but he managed to crawl to the distant light of a US army casualty clearing station, where he received treatment plus 'a Dixie of hot bully stew and a good tot of rum'. The battalion was in the area together with 2nd Highland Light Infantry and 2nd Cameron Highlanders as part of an ill-starred Allied attempt to reinforce local Social Revolutionary forces opposed to the Bolshevik regime. In the summer of 1919, the Royals were eventually withdrawn and arrived back at Leith on 18 June. With them they brought a short-barrelled Russian field gun which was captured at the village of Chamovo and was kept as a trophy of war by the battalion. Later it was moved to Glencorse and was refurbished in 1999–2000. To the 2/10th Royal Scots falls the honour of being the last of the regiment's Territorial battalions to be demobilised after the First World War.

It had been a curious war for a Territorial formation which had been raised in Bathgate as a cyclist battalion and had served in Scotland and Ireland on coastal defence duties before being sent to Russia. In August 1918 it sailed for Archangel, and for most of the men it must have been a dislocating experience. Not only were they unaware of the implications behind the deployment, but most them were soldiers who had already served in France and been medically downgraded. Nonetheless, in the face of the harsh northern Russian winter and apathy on the part of the local population, they maintained the regiment's high standards in an

EIGHT

THE SECOND WORLD WAR: GERMANY AND ITALY

Between 1914 and 1918 the Royals had served on every battle front except for the campaigns against Ottoman forces in Mesopotamia and against German forces and their local allies in East and West Africa. Seven soldiers had been awarded the Victoria Cross (see Appendix), the regiment had won 71 battle honours, of which 10 are borne on the colours and over 100,000 men had worn the Royal Scots cap badge. However, the price had been high in human terms. The Royals lost 583 officers and 10,630 men, and an estimated 40,000 soldiers had been wounded. Some of that last number would die later as a result of war-related wounds or illness. The end of hostilities also saw the dismantling of the huge military machine that had been constructed to fight Germany and its allies. All of the Royal Scots New Army battalions were disbanded and the Territorial battalions were either disbanded or re-formed. In 1922 the 4th and 5th battalions amalgamated as the 4/5th (Queen's Edinburgh) battalion and the 7th and 9th battalions amalgamated as the 7/9th (Highlanders) battalion. All the other wartime Territorial battalions were disbanded and the 3rd battalion was placed in a state of 'suspended animation' which allowed it to continue in being without having an operational existence. However, the regiment's wartime service was not forgotten. In 1922 the Royal Scots Memorial Club was opened in Abercromby Place in Edinburgh as a permanent and practical reminder of the regiment's sacrifices during the conflict. Five years later, a memorial gateway was opened at the regimental depot at Glencorse; it was consecrated 'To the Glorious Memory of those Royal Scots who, faithful unto death, gave their Lives for King and Country in the Great War 1914–1918'. Another milestone was passed in 1933 when the regiment and its friends celebrated the 300th anniversary of the formation of The Royal Scots.

For the regiment's two regular battalions, the return to peacetime soldiering also meant going back to familiar routines. After arriving in Edinburgh to re-form, the 1st battalion was deployed in Rangoon and served there and in India until the summer of 1926. Like the rest of the British Army, the Royals suffered from reductions in defence spending, but in 1936 the 1st battalion was converted to a mechanised role as a machine-gun battalion operating tracked carriers and 15 cwt trucks. In 1938 the battalion was ordered to move to Palestine, and returned to Britain the following January. During its deployment in Palestine it lost 15 killed and 42 wounded in the confrontation between Arabs and Zionist settlers.

For the 2nd battalion, the immediate post-war years were spent in Ireland on internal security duties during the war of independence which accompanied the transfer of power and partition of the country, and it was not finally withdrawn until 1922. Four years later, the battalion moved to Egypt for a posting which lasted until September 1928, when it was deployed in Tientsin in northern

China; one of its duties was to provide guards to the British Legation in Peking. It formed part of a garrison of 11,000 British and Indian troops, which was stationed in northern China to protect British interests and investments against attack by local warlords. After a deployment which one officer remembered for its pleasures, spending most of his time 'wandering all over the place, sightseeing, shopping and shooting', the battalion transferred to India in 1930 and served on the North-West Frontier and in the Punjab. Eight years later, in January 1938, the 2nd battalion moved further east to join the British garrison in Hong Kong.

One fact bound the two battalions together: like the rest of the British Army, they were unprepared for the war which broke out in September 1939 following the invasion of Poland by the German army. To wage a new global war the British Army could put together only four divisions as an expeditionary force for Europe, six infantry and one armoured division in the Middle East, a field division and a brigade in India, two brigades in Malaya and a modest scattering of imperial garrisons elsewhere. Years of neglect and tolerance of old-fashioned equipment meant that the army was ill-prepared to meet the modern German forces in battle, and British industry was not geared up to make good those deficiencies. Once again, it seemed that Britain was going to war with the equipment and mentality of previous conflicts. Events in Poland quickly showed that Germany was a ruthless and powerful enemy: the country fell within 18 days of the invasion, allowing the German leader, Adolf Hitler, to turn his attention to France. At the end of September 1939, as part of the deployment of British forces in France, the 1st battalion crossed the English Channel and landed at Cherbourg. From there it marched towards the Belgian border and took its place on the right of the British lines, in the area around Lecelles.

This was the period which came to be known as 'the phoney

war', and the lull in hostilities allowed the battalion to strike up friendships with the local population and units of the French Army, rekindling memories of the historic 'Auld Alliance' between France and Scotland. There was a change of sorts at Christmas, when the battalion moved into the French defensive positions of the Maginot Line, where it remained until the end of January 1940, but at that stage there was still no sign of any movement from the Germans. Back in their old positions at Lecelles, the Royals were put through a period of intensive training and live firing exercises in advance of the expected German onslaught. On 10 May, the war sprang into life again when Hitler's forces invaded Belgium and Holland and the 1st battalion moved up to Wavre, south of Brussels and close to the battlefield at Waterloo, where the 3rd battalion had fought over 100 years earlier. First contact with the enemy was made five days later, on the River Dyle, and in the face of a heavy German attack the battalion was forced to withdraw towards a new position near Calonne, and then further back towards Lys, scene of some of the fiercest fighting in 1918. It passed through a countryside rich with names that were redolent of the fighting in Flanders during that earlier conflict – Tournai, Armentières, Bailleul and Lille. This was a chaotic period for the British forces and, although the battalion was in continuous contact with the enemy, it was also involved in a desperate rearguard action which quickly degenerated into a full-scale retreat. As Augustus Muir described the situation, 'to look back on these days and nights afterwards was to enter a nightmare world'.

As the straggling remnants of the British Army fought their way back towards the Channel coast and to eventual evacuation from Dunkirk, on 27 May the Royals made their last stand at a position called Le Paradis, close to La Bassée Canal, another name familiar to the regiment. In the company of elements of The 2nd Royal Norfolk Regiment, they faced an overwhelming assault by superior German forces including armoured units, and within three days the battalion had fought itself to a standstill. Although some survivors managed to make their escape back to Britain through Dunkirk, the 1st battalion had ceased to exist as a coherent fighting unit. Amongst those who managed to escape was the commanding officer, Lieutenant-Colonel (later Brigadier) H.D.K. Money, who said later that:

> The Battalion did all that was asked of it; and the behaviour of all ranks was in the spirit of the highest traditions of the Regiment. Never once did the men fail to respond to their orders; never once did the Battalion give up a position until ordered to do so; and never did the men fail to respond to the old cry, 'Come on, The Royals!'

During the fighting in Belgium the battalion lost 141 dead and around 350 wounded, while 292 of its number went into German captivity.

It was not the regiment's final sally in Europe during those desperate weeks of 1940. The following month, having mobilised in September 1939 after the annual summer camp, the 7/9th battalion crossed over to France as part of the British reinforcements, which included 52nd (Lowland) Division, but after spending three days under attack near Le Mans it was evacuated to prevent a repetition of the disaster which had overwhelmed the British Army in Belgium. Fortunately, it suffered no casualties and returned to Britain relatively unscathed.

At the time, the evacuation of the shattered British Army at Dunkirk was hailed as a 'miracle' – 338,000 Allied soldiers made good their escape – but the new Prime Minister, Winston Churchill, got nearer to the truth when he said that 'never has a great nation been so naked before her foes'. For the Royals, the first task was to re-form the 1st battalion from those who had survived the fighting in Belgium and from 600 new recruits who had been called up for war service. Under the command of Lieutenant-Colonel A.J.L. Purvis, the battalion came back into being in Bradford in Yorkshire in the first weeks of June before going into divisional reserve as coastal defence troops in the area between Filey and Spurn Head. Later in the year there was a welcome return to offensive training when the battalion moved back to Scotland to practise amphibious operations on Loch Fyne. Back in Yorkshire, the battalion continued training throughout 1941 before moving to Glasgow on 15 April 1942 to join a troopship for deployment to an 'unknown destination' which turned out to be India. It was a long and tiring voyage which took them round the Cape of Good Hope, and they did not disembark in Bombay until 10 June. The rest of the 1st battalion's story is told in the next chapter.

As was the case in 1914, there was an immediate call for fresh soldiers, but this time the bulk of them were provided not by volunteers, as had happened in 1914, but by the introduction of conscription. The National Service (Armed Forces) Act of September 1939 made all able-bodied men between the ages of 18 and 41 liable for service 'for the duration of the hostilities', and within 3 months 727,000 had registered for service. Subsequent legislation brought in a total of 4.32 million conscripts to serve in the armed forces between 1941 and 1945. To meet the influx the army had to change, and in June 1940 the 50th (Holding) Battalion Royal Scots was formed to provide drafts for the regiment's regular and Territorial battalions. Based at Dreghorn Barracks in Edinburgh, it was redesignated 12th Royal Scots in October and was then posted to take part in coastal defence duties in north-east Scotland, Northumberland and the Shetland islands. Other changes had already affected the regiment. Prior to the outbreak of war, the 4/5th battalion had been converted into a Light Anti-Aircraft Regiment and served as 52nd Searchlight Regiment, Royal Artillery (Queen's Edinburgh Royal Scots) before becoming 130th Light Anti-Aircraft Regiment, Royal Artillery (Queen's Edinburgh Royal Scots); then in April 1939, as part of the expansion of the Territorial Army, the 8th (Lothians and Peeblesshire) battalion was re-formed. At the beginning of 1942, in a further change, the 12th battalion was disbanded and then re-formed immediately as the regiment's new 2nd battalion to take the place of the old 2nd battalion, which had been forced to surrender in Hong Kong the previous December. (The story is told in the next chapter.) In April 1943, the new 2nd battalion was then posted to Gibraltar, where it remained for over a year on garrison duties before moving to Italy in the summer of 1944 to take part in the final stages of the fighting against the retreating German army in the Apennines.

2ND BATTALION, ITALY, 1944–45

Following the decisive victories in North Africa and the capture of Sicily in the summer of 1943, Italy had been invaded by the British and US Allies in September. At the same time the Italians had surrendered, and while the Allies dithered over acceptance of the terms, the Germans moved 16 divisions into Italy to continue the war. These forces were to prove more than a handful to the Allies. Although landings at Salerno had been strongly opposed, the Allied armies had moved north from Naples, where they met fierce resistance along a defensive position known as the Gustav Line. The onset of winter and determined German resistance, particularly at Monte Cassino, had frustrated the Allies, who attempted to outflank the Germans by making a landing further north at Anzio. Once again the Germans refused to give ground and counter-attacked, with the result that the Allies struggled to gain any momentum and did not enter Rome until 5 June 1944.

Before they arrived in the city, the Germans withdrew north to the Apennines to complete a new defensive position, known as the Gothic Line. It was at this stage of the war that the 2nd battalion joined the 66th Infantry Brigade as part of the 1st Infantry Division in the Arno sector. (Originally, the brigade was to have joined the 1st Armoured Division.) The 2nd battalion was brigaded with 1st Hertfordshire Regiment and 11th Lancashire Fusiliers. Time had been set aside for training, but the need for troops meant that the Royals were in action north of Florence by the middle of August.

This phase of the operations kept the battalion in constant contact with the enemy as the former patrolled aggressively on the high ground on the northern side of the Arno following the fall of Florence and the withdrawal of German forces. Not only were the Royals facing a determined enemy but, as one of their number recalled in the regimental magazine after the war, they also had to confront difficult conditions on the ground:

> In the almost complete absence of tracks, all supplies had to be carried up by mules from a mule point which was continually moving up the Arrow Route [the road from Florence to Faenza] as the advance progressed, though even then the mule parties often had to cover 12 miles or more of appalling going in the dark, in trackless country, to catch up with the ever-advancing troops. As at all times four rifle companies had to be supplied, a large number of employed men of the Support and Headquarter Companies were needed to run the mule trains, and in fairness to them there were few occasions when the rations did not get through somehow.

As the Germans retreated, they booby-trapped the roads with mines and in the upper reaches of the mountains formidable defences had been constructed. It was not until the middle of September that the Royals were able to take part in a brigade attack on the enemy's positions on Monte Prefetto, and the action came as a welcome diversion following the difficult weeks of patrolling and isolated skirmishing. After two days of heavy fighting, Monte Prefetto was finally taken and the way was open to attack a neighbouring German stronghold on Monte Paganino, whose approaches proved to be 'both precipitous and slippery'. Adding to their problems underfoot, the weather worsened with the autumn rains and the Royals had to fight over tracks 'knee-deep in mud', and the position was not taken until 20 September. This took them over the Apennines, and as the brigade advanced northwards it was involved in further contact with the enemy at Presiola, Monte Gamberaldi, Monte Grande and Monte Castellaro. The last position was the only one which the brigade failed to take. As September gave way to October and November, the battalion found itself fighting over some of the worst terrain experienced by British soldiers during the war in Europe.

In January 1945 the 1st Division handed over the Monte Grande sector to the US 85th Division and started moving south to Taranto to embark on a new deployment in Palestine. On 26 January, they boarded the troopship *Bergensfiord* and sailed for Haifa, which was reached five days later. During the operations in Italy, the 2nd battalion's casualties were 2 officers and 40 soldiers killed, 12 officers and 114 soldiers wounded and 3 officers and 54 soldiers missing. The plan was to give the 1st Infantry Division a period of intensive training in river crossing and the use of armour before returning it to Italy in June, but the end of the war in Europe on 8 May put paid to that idea. The battalion remained in the Middle East until the end of 1946.

7/9th BATTALION, HOLLAND AND NORTH-WEST EUROPE, 1944–45

Following its brief foray into France with 52nd (Lowland) Division, the 7/9th battalion returned to Britain and was deployed briefly in an anti-invasion role in East Anglia. In October it moved back to Scotland, where the battalion spent almost a year at Alloa and then at Gullane in East Lothian, where it received new equipment. Following six months in the north-east of Scotland, the battalion started training with 52nd (Lowland) Division in its new and specialised role as mountain warfare troops, prior to an anticipated invasion of Norway. From autumn 1942, and throughout the following year, the battalion was involved in a series of arduous training exercises in the Cairngorms which involved the men living in the hills for weeks at a time. Instruction was given in fighting in snow conditions, skiing and handling of loads on horses and mules. For the men of the Royals it was an entirely new kind of training. According to Colonel F.L. Johnston, writing in *The Thistle* in January 1946:

> This had been arduous and exhausting, involving as it did the carrying of enormous loads over the peaks of the Cairngorms. All will remember Exercise 'Edelweiss', conducted in a two-day blizzard, and 'Goliaths I and II', which lasted two and three weeks respectively. On returning from our advanced training base at Derry Lodge it was a pleasant change to undergo training in combined operations at Inverary.

The move to the west coast gave the battalion the opportunity to train for amphibious operations but by then, the spring of 1944, it was clear that the invasion of Norway was no longer a priority. Instead, the division, including the 7/9th battalion, was given a new role as an air-transportable formation. The idea was to use the division in support of airborne operations by landing it with its own transport (jeeps and trailers) after parachute troops had secured the ground. It was an ambitious concept, and a number of potential targets were identified, including the Brest peninsula and the Forest of Rambouillet south of Paris, but the speed of the Allied advance after D-Day put paid to any of the plans being put into effect. A more ambitious plan to use the 52nd (Lowland) Division in support of the 1st Airborne's ill-fated operations at Arnhem also failed to materialise, for obvious reasons. Eventually, in the middle of October, the battalion was re-rolled again, this time as an ordinary infantry formation when the 52nd (Lowland) Division was given the task of opening the port of Antwerp under the operational command of the First Canadian Army. For the men of the Royals it was 'a curious and ironic twist of fate that the Battalion, after all its long years of training to fight on the mountain-tops and being carried to war through the air, should eventually become involved in an amphibious operation below sea level, but this is in fact what happened and on 3rd November 1944, the Battalion was launched in the assault on Flushing' (Colonel F.L. Johnston, writing in *The Thistle*). The Royals had not been in the area since 1809, when the 3rd battalion took part in the operations on the island of Walcheren.

At this stage of the war, the Allies had successfully completed the D-Day landings which had begun the invasion of Europe, and had broken out of Normandy. However, the speed and aggression of their advance had produced enormous problems of supply and re-supply – the further they advanced into Europe, the further away were the main Channel ports which provided them with much-needed fuel, munitions and the matériel of war. The one port capable of giving them everything they needed was Antwerp, with its huge docks, but it was still in German control and its seaward approaches were heavily mined. With winter approaching, the need to capture Antwerp and open up the Scheldt estuary was imperative, and so it was that the mountain soldiers of the 52nd (Lowland) Division found themselves crossing the Channel in the middle of October to support Canadian forces in a part of Europe that was below sea level. The 7/9th battalion landed at Ostend and regrouped in the nearby town of Waereghem, where it was given a hero's welcome and offered tremendous hospitality. Its first objective was Flushing, in Walcheren, which the Germans had earmarked as the key to open the Scheldt estuary and had reinforced accordingly.

The Royals went into action on the last day of October, landing in Flushing by landing-craft and finding themselves quickly caught up in the difficult and dangerous business of fighting in a built-up area. Faced by the onslaught, the Germans put up determined resistance and fought stubbornly to protect their positions. There was no fiercer battle than the struggle to take the Grand Hotel Britannia, which stood on the outskirts of Flushing and which turned out to be the headquarters of the German garrison. Before the attack began, the Royals thought that the building contained no more than 50 Germans, but it soon became clear that it was a major target. According to the war history of the 52nd (Lowland) Division, 'it was obvious that the enemy was holding this locality in considerable strength'. When the Royals attacked, the Germans set the building on fire and maintained a stout resistance with machine-gun and rifle fire:

> Opposition was strong, nearly all the buildings were
> occupied by snipers; a machine-gun and a 20 mm were
> sited on the roof of the hotel, and the surrounding
> buildings were completely ringed by a concrete trench

system and the Germans covered all approaches to the hotel. It was quite impossible to call for [artillery] fire support since our troops were so closely engaged with the enemy.

By the end of the day on 3 November the hotel had been taken by the 7/9th battalion, and Flushing was in Allied hands. During the action, the Royals lost three officers and fifteen soldiers killed and one officer and forty-nine soldiers wounded.

The next stage of the operations in Walcheren was the attack on the German headquarters in the town of Middleburg, which lay to the north and had been flooded after the Allies bombarded its sea dykes. This was taken by the battalion in an audacious attack using 'Buffalo' amphibious vehicles, which raced into the town, taking the Germans by complete surprise. There followed some spirited negotiations with the enemy commander, who was told that unless he surrendered, Middleburg would be destroyed by aerial bombing and artillery fire. Although 'in no affable mood' the German General Daser agreed to an immediate ceasefire in the belief that he had been surrounded and captured by superior forces. This was far from true, but the Royals' senior officer Major R.H.B. Johnstone maintained the pretence; when a German officer tried to point out the discrepancy, the battalion's interpreter, a Norwegian officer, 'with great presence of mind shut him up and hustled him from the room before he could do much damage'. The Royals' losses were six killed and six wounded. The capture of Middleburg allowed the Scheldt estuary to reopen to Allied shipping, and the first transport ships were able to enter Antwerp by the end of November.

The battalion's next operation was the advance towards the Rhine which would take it through Holland and into Germany under the operational command of the Second British Army.

At the beginning of December it crossed over the border into Germany near Geilenkirchen. Its first major operation of the new year was an assault on the enemy bridgehead at the well-defended town of Heinsberg, a place that reminded one of the Royals' officers of Haddington, in East Lothian. The attack was made in conjunction with 4th King's Own Scottish Borderers. By 24 January, the position had been taken and, in Augustus Muir's words, 'If the Jocks required anything to fire their ardour they could derive it from the reflection that they had been given the job of attacking the largest town yet to be captured by the Allies.' The next phase of the operation saw the 7/9th battalion advancing steadily into German territory, often under heavy shellfire, and having to tackle minefields as they approached the southern edge of the Reichswald Forest. Between 17 and 23 February the battalion was involved in a difficult brigade attack on Kasteel Blijenbeek, a medieval fortress which had to be approached through the thick woodlands. The Germans put up strong resistance, and eventually the objective was destroyed by Allied air power. During this testing time the Royals faced an intensive period of artillery bombardment, which was reflected in the 44 casualties killed or wounded during the operation.

From there the battalion moved up to the Rhine, where the 52nd (Lowland) Division was tasked with helping with the preparations for the crossing which would take the British forces into the north German plain. The end of the war was now in sight, and after the capture of the Dortmund-Ems Canal at the beginning of April, the brigade containing the battalion (155th Brigade) was put under the operational command of the 7th Armoured Division, the famed 'Desert Rats', who had made their name fighting under General Montgomery in North Africa in 1942. In a letter written to the Colonel of the Regiment (Colonel J.H. Mackenzie), the battalion's commanding officer Lieutenant-Colonel J.G. Dawson provided an exhilarating picture of the 7/9th's activities during that final thrust into German territory:

> Everyone, apart from the natural dislike of battle itself, thoroughly enjoyed their time with the Armour and we were awfully glad to have stayed with them so long. They were stirring times and length of advances were sometimes amazing. It was an odd feeling at times to find oneself sitting in a car motoring perhaps 60 miles through Germany, knowing full well that only the road itself, and perhaps a quarter of a mile on either side of it, had been cleared the day before. We were, of course, mainly used to clear up pockets on the axis that the Armour had by-passed, and on the flanks.

After being involved in the attack on Soltau, where the Germans put up stout resistance, the brigade returned to its parent division to take part in the assault on Bremen which began on 23 April. For the battalion, the war ended in the village of Worpeswede by the River Elbe when the bugler sounded 'Cease Fire' on the morning of 5 May, leaving Colonel Dawson to ponder 'what lay ahead of us, the clearing-up of the great destruction and the disorganisation of human life that war brought in its train'. The battalion remained in Germany until the following year, and was disbanded at Detmold on 26 June 1946. When the Territorial Army was re-formed on 1 May 1947 the 7/9th battalion was reconstituted, with its headquarters in East Claremont Street, Edinburgh.

8TH BATTALION, FRANCE, HOLLAND AND NORTH-WEST EUROPE, 1944–45

After re-forming in Scotland in August 1939 with recruits from Edinburgh, the Lothians and Peeblesshire (including the entire St Ronan's Silver Band) the 8th battalion became part of the 15th (Scottish) Division, and its first wartime service was on anti-invasion duties in southern England before returning north for more advanced training in Northumberland and then in Yorkshire. This involved cooperation with armoured formations in preparation for the invasion of Europe, and the long months of hard training and waiting came to an end in May when the 15th (Scottish) Division moved down to the Channel coast. On 11 June, a week after the D-Day landings in which the Royals' affiliated regiment, the Canadian Scottish Regiment, had participated, the 8th battalion crossed over to France, the troops sailing from Newhaven and the transport from Tilbury docks in London. Within days of arriving, it made its first contact with the enemy when the battalion was involved in the first phase of Operation Epsom, which began on 26 June. The area they fought over was known as the 'Scottish Corridor'.

In his study of the fighting after D-Day, *Six Armies in Normandy*, John Keegan makes the point that although this was the division's first experience of war 'in actuality', the Territorial battalions all had great traditions and 'encapsulated the whole of Scottish military history' with the 8th battalion 'belonging by association to Hepburn's Regiment, which had tramped the campaigning fields of Germany in the service of France during the Thirty Years War'. Keegan argues that they were 'innocents to war inasmuch as Scots can ever be', but in the hours and days that lay ahead they would need all that history and resilience to see them through some of the fiercest fighting during the break-out from the Normandy beach-head. Their objective was the high ground to the east of the River Orne, between Caen and Falaise, and to clear the enemy from the flanks. It was a bruising experience: at Haut du Bosq the battalion headquarters were almost overrun and at one point A Company was reduced to 30 men for the defence of the right flank. All told, the division suffered 2,500 casualties and the battalion lost 20 officers and 431 soldiers killed, but in the words of one of the men who took part in the operation, 'after that first blooding, the Battalion and the Division were made' (quoted in *The Thistle*, April 1946). The advance continued until the end of the month, when the battalion enjoyed a short period of respite at Tourmauville. At this time they were joined by an Australian officer, Major Henry Gullett, who left an attractive snapshot of the battalion in his memoirs *Not Only as Duty: An Infantryman's War*:

> Both the men and its officers were Scots, sharing pride in Scotland's history, her glory and her music. The officers were no less proud of their Scottishness than the troops were. They sang the same songs, danced to the same pipe music, played the same games, shared memories of home.

The fighting in the Scottish Corridor continued until the third week of July, when the battalion moved on to the next phase of the fighting, the advance to the Escaut Canal. On 28 August, the Royals crossed the Seine and began the advance towards the frontier with Belgium which became, in the words of the regimental historian 'a triumphal procession rather than a phase of war'. Hard fighting returned in the middle of September, when the battalion was involved in the operations to secure bridgeheads over the Escaut Canal near the village of Aart. This meant advancing towards the objective during the night of 13 September and beginning the attack at dawn. The Germans put up fierce resistance, and the fighting continued for three days, leaving the battalion with 163 casualties: it was referred to later as the Battle of the Gheel Bridgehead. Despite the losses and the battalion's exhaustion, the advance had to continue, and by 22 September the 8th battalion reached Eindhoven in Holland. At Fratershoef the fighting was stopped for an hour on 28 September when the commanding officer, Lieutenant-Colonel Lane-Joynt, agreed to a local truce with his German opposite number to allow the wounded to be brought in under white flag. The fighting began again the next day, but, as noted in Augustus Muir's *The First of Foot*, one officer in the battalion never forgot such a rare occurrence in warfare:

> It was a blessed relief to have an hour of peace after some most unpleasant shelling. At the end of the hour punctually to the second, one shell was fired from the German side. Clearly it was not meant to hit anything and not another shot was fired by either side for the remainder of that Thursday night. The whole episode impressed me as an odd little bit of chivalry, and we appreciated it.

After Fratershoef the 15th (Scottish) Division handed over to the 51st (Highland) Division and went into reserve. The 8th battalion's next battle was in support of the attack on the town of Tilburg, which was itself part of an operation to support the attack on the Scheldt in which the 7/9th battalion was involved. Early in December, with armoured support, the battalion was again involved in heavy fighting during the capture of Blerick, and spent the next two months preparing for the crossing of the Rhine. This period provided it with its last set-piece battle of the war, the battle for the town of Goch, which the historian of

44th Brigade was moved to call 'perhaps the finest performance of The Royal Scots in the war'. As A Company approached the town it was thought to be lightly defended, but that reckoning was quickly altered by the Germans, who responded to the attack with heavy mortar and machine-gun fire. It was not until the following day that the northern part of Goch was taken and there was 'some tough fighting before those resolute enemy troops were ejected from the town'. In the days that followed, the battalion was engaged in equally hard fighting on the high ground overlooking Schloss Kalbeck. The battalion's losses during February were 26 killed and 115 wounded.

On 23–24 March, the battalion had the distinction of being one of the first formations to cross the Rhine in amphibious Buffalo vehicles, the task of 44th Brigade being to link up with the airborne forces which had been dropped to the east. Once again, the Germans offered fierce resistance, but Germany's western frontier was finally breached and the end of the war was in sight. As the commander of 44th Brigade put it in a signal to the battalion, the day had been an unalloyed success:

> When the Commanding Officer of The Royal Scots and the Lowland Brigade Commander drove up shortly afterwards to the Brigade Headquarters of the Parachute Brigade, there was an enthusiastic scene, the parachutists crowding round to cheer the Scotsmen who had fought through to their relief.
>
> The day ended triumphantly. The Lowlanders had stormed the Rhine, captured 1,000 German prisoners and many guns, relieved the airborne troops and opened up the way for the breakthrough. The casualties had not been light, but the soldiers were in tremendous spirits.

From the Rhine, the battalion moved towards Hanover and another river crossing, the Elbe, on 29 April which the commanding officer, Lieutenant-Colonel Barclay Pearson, found 'harder and more unpleasant than the Rhine'. A week later came the ceasefire. During almost a year of continuous fighting in Europe the 8th battalion had lost 97 officers and 1,151 soldiers killed, a figure which is put in perspective by considering that the war establishment of a British infantry battalion was 37 officers and 845 soldiers. The battalion ended its service near Bad Bramstadt near the demarcation line with the Soviet zone and it was disbanded at Bergesdorf on 11 March, with the final church parade taking place six days later. When the Territorial Army was re-formed in May 1947, the 8th battalion was reconstituted with its battalion headquarters in Dalkeith to the south-east of Edinburgh.

NINE

THE SECOND WORLD WAR: JAPAN

Japan entered the war on Sunday, 7 December 1941, with its infamous pre-emptive air strike on the US Pacific Fleet's base at Pearl Harbor in Hawaii. This was followed in quick succession by further Japanese attacks on the islands of Guam, Wake and Midway while the Japanese Second Fleet escorted General Tomoyoku Yamashita's Twenty-Fifth Army to attack the north-west coast of the Malay peninsula. For the British this was a valuable asset, as it produced almost 40 per cent of the world's rubber and 58 per cent of the world's tin; it was also the key to Britain's major naval base at Singapore. At the same time, three Japanese divisions prepared to invade the British colony of Hong Kong in southern China. This vital port and trading centre had been in British hands since 1842, when it was ceded by the Treaty of Nanking as an open port. In 1860 further territory was acquired on the mainland at Kowloon, and under the Peking Convention of 1898 the New Territories were taken over from China under a 99-year lease. As a British Crown Colony Hong Kong prospered, as it offered a secure and dependable base during a period of upheaval which included the fall of the Manchu dynasty and Japanese intervention in China's internal affairs. It was, though, something of a strategic backwater, and at the outbreak of the Second World War its defences were pitiful. In the event of enemy attack, the civil and military authorities had simply been told to hang on for as long as possible as there was no hope of any help or reinforcement. The question of Hong Kong's position was put into stark relief by Winston Churchill on 7 January 1941 when he rejected the idea of sending reinforcements as 'there is not the slightest chance of holding Hong Kong or relieving it . . . we must avoid frittering away our resources on untenable positions'.

As a result, in the summer of 1941, the land forces element of the Hong Kong garrison consisted of two British battalions, 2nd Royal Scots and 2nd Middlesex Regiment (a machine-gun battalion), and two Indian battalions, 5/7th Rajput Regiment and 2/14th Punjab Regiment. These were supported by local artillery and volunteer defence units, but they were modestly equipped and trained. Two raw Canadian militia battalions arrived in November but, apart from adding numbers and increasing morale, their arrival only reinforced Churchill's warning about frittering away resources. The naval and air forces were also meagre – one destroyer, eight motor torpedo boats, four gunboats and seven obsolescent reconnaissance aircraft. In short, the regiment's historian of the Second World War is entirely correct in stating that 'Hong Kong was a "hostage to fortune" and it fell before the Japanese onslaught on Christmas Day 1941'. However, that bald and historically accurate statement does not tell the whole story of the valiant attempt to defend an impossible position, and the suffering which was visited on those who survived the short but fiercely fought battle for Hong Kong.

2ND BATTALION (OLD), HONG KONG, 1941

The 2nd Royal Scots had arrived in Hong Kong in January 1938 following a lengthy deployment in India and, according to Augustus Muir, they quickly felt at home in a place where Scottish voices were familiar in the trading community and where 'they could hear that most familiar of noises of the Auld Reekie [Edinburgh] of that time – the clank of jolting tramcars'. The scenery, too, was pleasing and the atmosphere within the colony was vibrant and exotic. For officers and men alike, Hong Kong was an ideal posting, with its sporting and social opportunities, and a climate which provided hot summers and mild and refreshing autumn and winter days. As for training, it was pursued enthusiastically but as Hong Kong was low on the army's priorities it proved difficult to keep the battalion up to scratch. When the 2nd battalion arrived in Hong Kong it was supposed to convert its role to become a machine-gun formation, but shortages of Lewis guns put paid to that initiative. Shortly after arriving in the colony the Royals reverted to operating as a rifle battalion, with four rifle companies and a headquarter company consisting of mortar, pioneer, intelligence, anti-aircraft, signal and administrative platoons. The battalion responded quickly and efficiently to the changes, but unit cohesion was not helped by the fact that it was spread over four separate barracks with some elements operating on the mainland. During those difficult early days of the war it also proved hard to hold onto key personnel: all too often, experienced officers, warrant officers and non-commissioned officers were posted out of Hong Kong to serve in other units or training establishments elsewhere. As a result, when the battalion went to war it had only four regular officers and the commanding officer, Lieutenant-Colonel S.E.H.E. White, took over command only a matter of weeks before the Japanese attack began.

To add to the difficulties in retaining personnel, there had been a last-minute revision of the defence plan occasioned by the arrival of the two Canadian battalions. Already there had been a number of proposals, ranging from manning a secure defensive 'inner line' on the mainland to a more limited plan to deploy mobile forces on the mainland before pulling back to the island. Shortages of manpower and equipment meant that the defence of the mainland positions was always going to be a problem, and by the outbreak of hostilities its pill-boxes, weapons pits and trenches had been largely abandoned. However, for all that the defence of the mainland was considered a non-starter, the plan was put into effect by the colony's new garrison commander, Major-General C.M. Maltby, General Officer Commanding, China Command. Under his revised plan, three battalions would form a new brigade, which would be responsible for defending the positions on the mainland. These would be the Royals, the Rajputs and the Punjabis, while the Canadians and the Middlesex took up defensive positions on the island of Hong Kong. Astonishingly, right up to the last minute, Maltby believed that the inner lines on the mainland could be held for up to seven days, even though intelligence reports revealed that the attacking Japanese forces would number up to 20,000 troops. The thinking behind Maltby's plan was plain – to provide a first line of defence which would give the colony some breathing space and the opportunity to destroy key installations – but it failed to take into account the disastrous state of the physical defences and the fact that the positions were supposed to be held by a full infantry division. Unhappily, like many other senior army officers of his generation, Maltby had a low regard for the military abilities of the Japanese, and held to the view that they would be unable to compete against Western soldiers – among the many absurd misapprehensions was a widely accepted belief that they were incapable of fighting at night. There was even optimism that the Japanese were bluffing, and that the expected attack on Hong Kong would fail to materialise. During the weekend when war broke out in the East, no one saw any reason to cancel parties or dances in Hong Kong and church parade was held as usual on the day (7 December) that Pearl Harbor was attacked.

For the Royals, the move into Lo Wu Camp on the mainland had come as an unpleasant surprise. Not only was the change ordered a bare three weeks before the Japanese attack began, but they soon discovered that many of the positions were, in Muir's words, 'at best, makeshift'. As described by Captain David Pinkerton, the Royals' sector lay to the north-west of Kowloon and from the left, it:

> . . . ran from the sea across the valley between the Tai Mo Shan and Golden Hill ranges up to the Shingmun Redoubt, a miniature fortress of pill-boxes and concrete trenches communicating with each other by underground passages. The redoubt stood on the forward slope of a knife-edged ridge, overlooking a reservoir, on the far side of which the middle slopes of Tai Mo Shan rise up to its summit. From this point, the Inner Line slanted backwards, so that the redoubt was the apex of an angle facing the enemy, and obviously a key point.

The lie of the land would have been known to many of the men, as the mainland was used for annual training exercises, but the battalion was now forced to put itself onto a war footing in a tactical position which was unfamiliar to them. For a start, the positions had to be renovated. Pill-boxes had to be cleaned out and new trenches had to be dug. Wiring had to be replaced, communications enhanced and minefields created, although the last activity was hampered by an acute shortage of anti-personnel mines. One fact stands for many: the key position was thought to be the Shing Mun Redoubt, yet it was manned by 42 soldiers, consisting of A Company headquarters (one officer and nine soldiers), an artillery observation post (one officer and four soldiers) and one officer and twenty-six soldiers of 8 Platoon. All-told, the Royals were expected to hold a defensive line which stretched over 5,000 yards, five times the recommended minimum. The only artillery support came from 16 howitzers and from the 6-inch guns of the gunboat HMS *Cicala*. Other than the name of the defences – Gin Drinker's Line – there was not much to smile about, although with typical resolve, Pinkerton noted his belief that on the eve of battle 'we felt we were quite prepared to receive the Japanese'.

The 2nd battalion's war began on 8 December at dawn, on what many soldiers remembered as a perfect Hong Kong winter's morning, crisp and sunny. As the Japanese air force flew missions to attack and destroy the RAF base at Kai Tak airfield, the Japanese army's 38th Division, commanded by Lieutenant-General Sano Tadayoshi, crossed the Sam Chun River into the Leased Territories and by the following day had reached the main defensive line. Despite determined resistance from the Royals, the Shing Mun Redoubt quickly fell into enemy hands and its loss made the already over-extended defensive lines untenable. Much to Maltby's anger and disappointment, there was no option but to order withdrawal from the mainland, and the operation was completed on 13 December. During this initial phase of the battle, the Royals lost 99 casualties, most of them in D Company, which had begun the battle with 70 men and lost 16 killed and 17 wounded. Amongst the survivors was 2nd Lieutenant James Allan Ford, who remembered that 'after all the Battalion had come through we left the battlefield in buses, as if we were going back to the barracks after an exercise in the hills'. Later still, after the war, Ford became a distinguished writer and his novel *The Brave*

White Flag (1961) is his own comment on the tragedy of the fall of Hong Kong.

Once back on the island of Hong Kong the options facing the defenders were limited, although, once again, the resistance was determined and whole-hearted. In the opening rounds, the Japanese bombarded defensive positions and launched air attacks on Victoria, the central business district. During this phase the 2nd battalion was deployed in the north-east sector until 16 December, when it handed over to the Rajputs and went into reserve. Two days later, the Japanese landed in strength between North Point and Aldrich Bay and moved quickly to bisect the island and split the defending forces. To do this, they had to take possession of the strategically important Wong Nei Chong Gap, which guarded the main north–south road at the narrowest point in the island, but the importance of the feature was ignored by Maltby. Later, this failure to reinforce the position was condemned in the Official War History, as it 'resulted in the enemy being able to reach this vital point without encountering any serious opposition'. It also meant that the 2nd battalion found itself caught up in some of the fiercest fighting on the island. Despite determined attempts to clear Japanese positions on 19 December, the Royals were forced to withdraw from a hopeless situation, and one subaltern spoke for everyone in the battalion when he said: 'That was the worst day my men had in all the Hong Kong fighting, and as an officer in battle, the worst day I experienced.'

The ferocity displayed by the defenders forced the Japanese to halt temporarily to regroup, but by then the end was already in sight. Casualties had been high on the Allied side, and with food, water and ammunition running low it was obvious that the ability to resist had been eroded. By 23 December, White was left with barely 180 men under his command and was unable to maintain contact with garrison headquarters other than by runner. And yet in spite of all the difficulties, some sparks of hope remained. On Christmas Eve, the arrival of 200 pairs of brown gym shoes allowed the battalion to mount night patrols with some hope of success, Pinkerton noting that 'by now it had become obvious that our patrols could do little useful work at night on roads or the stony hillsides in ammunition boots'. By contrast, the 'un-soldierly' Japanese had worn rubber-soled boots to good advantage. That proved to be the final piece of resistance. In the afternoon of Christmas Day, Maltby gave the order to surrender and to fly the white flag. For the Royals this came as shattering news, as they had been preparing themselves to fight to the last man, but Colonel White was forced to go forward to the Japanese lines through Wanchai Gap to give his surrender to the Japanese at the Hong Kong Tramway Depot at North Point. When the roll-call was taken, it was found that in the course of 17 days' fighting the Royals had lost 12 officers and 95 soldiers killed and 17 officers and 213 soldiers wounded.

The fighting for Hong Kong was over, but it was not the end of the war for the survivors, 22 officers and 608 soldiers, who went into Japanese captivity. For them, the four years as prisoners of war was to be a terrible experience and three officers and fifty-nine soldiers died whilst in Japanese hands. The treatment meted out to Allied prisoners of war has been well documented – for example, the high casualties on the Burma–Siam railway or the Bataan death march – but the Royals had further reason to be shocked by Japanese barbarity. After the fall of Hong Kong 1,816 British prisoners of war were transported to Japan on board the elderly freighter *Lisbon Maru*. As happened on many other 'death ships', they were packed into the holds where the average space for one man was one square yard, which meant sleeping in shifts and limited availability of latrines. On the night of 30 September 1942, the *Lisbon Maru* was attacked and torpedoed in the China

Sea by the submarine USS *Grouper*. Although the ship did not sink immediately, the British prisoners of war were battened down in the holds while most of the Japanese crew and guards were taken off. Two days later, with conditions worsening and the ship in danger of sinking, there was a mass break-out which ended in tragedy. Prisoners who jumped into the sea were drowned or used as target practice by the Japanese ships, and the rest failed to escape before the *Lisbon Maru* sank. Of the 1,816 who had set sail for Japan, only 970 survived and were taken to Japan, where they endured further misery in Japanese camps. It was not the worst incident – a fortnight earlier 5,620 Allied prisoners had been killed when a British submarine sank a larger freighter – but it does mean that the name *Lisbon Maru* occupies an unhallowed place in the regiment's history.

One other incident stands out from that desperate period. Many of the surviving Royals were placed in a camp at Sham Shui Po on the mainland, where they were commanded by their senior officer, Captain Douglas Ford. Early on, he managed to make contact with Chinese collaborators who had succeeded in smuggling in badly needed medical supplies. Plans were also made for a mass break-out, although the weakened condition of the men inside the camp made this something of a non-starter. In any case, as Ford's brother, James Allan Ford, has pointed out, 'the outward messages contained little, if anything, more than the International Red Cross would have learned, if Japan had been a signatory to the Geneva Convention'. But it was always a high-risk gamble, and when the Japanese discovered the extent of the communication, reprisals were inevitable. Along with others, Captain Ford was arrested on 10 July 1943 and subjected to sadistic torture and held in solitary confinement on starvation rations. Throughout the experience he refused to give anything away, despite receiving agonising treatment from his captors, and continued to accept sole responsibility for his actions. As a result, two sergeants implicated in the plot received prison sentences instead of the death penalty when the trials for espionage were held in December, but after perfunctory proceedings Ford and two other officers were condemned to death for committing an act of espionage. On 18 December they were shot by firing squad but even in those last dreadful minutes Ford's courage and resolution never wavered. Although weakened himself, he gave assistance to his brother officers, and as the junior of the three took his place on the left of the line. In acknowledgement of Ford's courage, the Japanese officer in charge of the firing squad insisted that the condemned man, a gallant Royal Scot, should stand on the right. After the war, Ford received the posthumous award of the George Cross 'in recognition of his most conspicuous gallantry while a prisoner of war in Japanese hands'.

1ST BATTALION, BURMA, 1943–45

The fall of Hong Kong and the later fall of Singapore on 15 February 1943 were followed by the collapse of British power in Burma and the threat that India itself might be invaded. Although invasion of India had not been part of the original intention of the Japanese attack, their armed forces had won such a convincing victory in Burma that there seemed to be no reason why India should not fall equally cheaply. In July 1942, the Japanese high command made plans for 'Operation 21', a three-pronged attack from Burma towards Ledo, Imphal and Chittagong. It was over-ambitious, as the terrain in northern Burma was not suited to rapid offensive operations, but the fact that India was threatened was enough to concentrate British minds about the precariousness of their position. Allied to increasingly noisy demands from Indian nationalists for Britain to quit India, there was an immediate need to restore British standing by taking the offensive back to the Japanese and retrieving lost ground in Burma. The first of these initiatives was the first Arakan campaign, which opened in September 1942 and which was aimed at capturing the Akyab peninsula following an advance from Chittagong by way of Cox's Bazaar and Donbaik. By the following May, the Japanese had retrieved all the ground won during the advance; for the British it was not only an expensive failure which cost over 5,000 casualties, but it inculcated a belief that the Japanese were unbeatable jungle fighters.

Amongst those taking part in the operation were 1st Royal Scots, who fought in 6th Independent Brigade Group together with 1st Royal Welch Fusiliers, 1st Royal Berkshire Regiment and 2nd Durham Light Infantry. Originally, the formation's role was to attack Akyab from the sea, an undertaking that involved the Royals in their first experience of combined operations, but shortages of landing craft necessitated a change of plan to more conventional operations. As a result, the Royals went into the line on 6 March 1943 for the attack on Donbaik, and the subsequent fighting gave them their first experience of taking on the Japanese, who had created heavily fortified positions in 'chaungs', river beds or deep tidal creeks. The Royals' commanding officer, Lieutenant-Colonel R.W. Jackson, originally a Sherwood Forester, provided a telling description of these obstacles (the article was written for *The Thistle* in conjunction with the battalion Intelligence Officer Captain J.S Purves):

> The position held by the Jap here [near Donbaik] was a small strong-point made out of the main chaung (or river bed) stretching from the sea to hills 500 to 800 feet high. These hills overlooked the chaung and were held by the Jap. The chaung itself was well dug, revetted sufficiently to withstand shelling from 25-pdrs or 3.7 howitzers.

It also included some tanks sunk into the ground. Our lines approached in places as close as 40 yards and gave the Battalion an inkling of what trench warfare used to be like, as part of the Battalion perimeter ran through a narrow chaung.

The description presaged the kind of fighting which followed. Despite facing heavy incoming fire, the Japanese showed that their positions were well defended and, as Jackson and Purves confirmed, 'a period of trench warfare set in'. One Japanese pill-box, known as 'Sugar 5', proved to be particularly impervious to attack and for a time the Royals were involved in an attempt to dig a mineshaft underneath it. An order to 'straighten the line' put paid to their efforts when 6th Brigade pulled back and 'angry and disgusted, the miners left their work uncompleted'. On 27 March the Brigade Group was ordered to move back to the north along the coastal plain, and during fierce fighting at Indin on 6 April the battalion suffered heavy casualties in an action which an officer described later as 'utter pandemonium'. During the Japanese attack on the brigade headquarters Brigadier R.V.C. Cavendish was killed and crucial documents, including codebooks, fell into enemy hands. There was no option for the Royals but to withdraw towards Kyaukpandu, where there was a chance to regroup. By then the first rains of the monsoon had begun and marching was difficult, with the result that 'most of us were sleeping on our feet . . . we looked like ragamuffins'.

The loss of the Buthiadaung-Maungdaw defensive line and the subsequent withdrawal were counted as victories for the Japanese, whose forces, commanded by Lieutenant-General Takeshi Koga, had shown dash and determination in their counter-attack, but as the battalion moved back towards the frontier, Captain Purves remembered that many of the men thought that 'we should have been going *south* against the Jap and not *north*'. Nevertheless, the retreat continued and the battalion moved back into India on 24 May. In the aftermath of the failure of the operation, the British high command criticised many of the front-line units for their lack of fighting spirit and willingness to surrender when facing heavy odds. During the latter stages of the campaign, a staff officer on the headquarters of Lieutenant-General N.M.S. Irwin reported that most of the infantrymen were 'either exhausted or browned-off or both' and were 'obviously scared of the Jap and generally demoralised by the nature of the campaign' or 'hate the country and see no object in fighting for it, and also have the strong feeling that they are taking part in a forgotten campaign in which no one in authority is taking any real interest'. The report was written after a visit to the brigades fighting on the Maungdaw Front in the second week of May, but the author of the report made an exception of the 6th Brigade 'who had had a hammering, but were still staunch'. During this first Arakan campaign the Royals' casualties were 6 officers and 26 soldiers killed and 10 officers and 117 soldiers wounded. Another 500 had fallen victim to malaria, with the result that when the battalion finally reached Chittagong it numbered only some 400 soldiers.

Once back in India, the battalion was moved to Ahemednagar, near Bombay, where it became part of 4th Infantry Brigade in 2nd Division, a 'formidable force' according to Louis Allen, a recent historian of the Burma campaign. The first task was to deal with the malaria which had caused so many casualties; the second was to embark on intensified training for jungle warfare. In January 1944 the battalion moved again, this time to Belgaum on the dry Deccan plateau in preparation for the next phase of the fighting in Burma. This proved to be a crucial period in the development of the battalion's fighting capabilities. Together with every other regiment of the British Army serving in the Burma theatre of operations, the Royals were given intensive training in how to survive in the jungle. Much of this had been gleaned from the practical experiences of Major-General Orde Wingate's Chindit forces, whose experimental long-range penetration operations had taken the war to the Japanese in Burma the previous year. As a result of Wingate's morale-boosting initiatives, British soldiers began to realise that they could fight in the jungle on equal terms with the Japanese, and that they could beat an enemy previously thought to be 'super-human'. In the words of Augustus Muir, the Royals were taught that 'the jungle is your best friend . . . you can live in the jungle, and you can live on the jungle – in the jungle you will find all you need to keep alive. There will of course be many dangers, but they need not get you down . . . As for the Japs in the jungle, you can beat them at their own game'.

The opportunity to put this new training into practice came in the spring of 1944, when the Japanese under General Renya Mutaguchi opened a major offensive across the River Chindwin to attack Imphal and Kohima in Assam. This would give the Japanese the springboard to invade India, and for that reason it was imperative for the British and Indian forces not just to hold those two key points but also the railhead at Dimapur, which was the end of the supply line from India. In the middle of April, the 1st battalion was flown into the area and landed at Dimapur and Jorhat where it went straight into the fighting, and first contact with the enemy was made on 19 April. It was a desperate situation. At the time, Kohima was garrisoned by a single battalion (4th Royal West Kent Regiment), together with some details of the Assam Rifles, and the initiative was firmly with the Japanese as the British took up their positions close to the town. For the Royals, this involved sending out fighting patrols against the enemy, and they soon found that it was going to be a long and wearisome experience. Writing after the war in *The Thistle*, the adjutant Captain F.C.

Currie recalled that although the jungle training came into its own, it was still difficult to pin down and kill the enemy:

> The Japs were well dug in on a steep cliff. We could not see them, but they could see us. We probed all round them, lost about a dozen men and then the Company withdrew. Our losses had not been heavy, but we had the unsatisfactory feeling that we had lost some very good men, and we could not swear to having killed a single Jap. It was our first attempt to turn the little yellow rats out of their holes without supporting fire, and our last. Just another jungle warfare lesson learnt and, all things considered, it was cheap at the price. It had no effect on our morale, but it made us very cross indeed.

Following several more equally tough encounters, the Royals moved westwards and began the slow slog of clearing the Japanese from their positions around Kohima. Some of the fiercest fighting took place at positions known as Pavilion Hill, GPT Ridge, Aradura Spur and the Pimple. Throughout this phase, the battalion was given tremendous help by the local Naga hill-men, who acted as porters and provided nothing but loyal and unstinting service. Kohima was a hard and unyielding battle which tested the Royals to the full, but the tenacity and courage of the British and Indian forces paid off on 31 May, when the Japanese began to withdraw. The decision was taken – against orders – by the Japanese commander, Lieutenant-General Kotuku Sato, to save his forces from 'futile annihilation', and it brought to an end 64 days of fighting which left the Japanese with 6,000 casualties and the British and Indian forces with 4,000 casualties. During that period the Royals lost 1 officer and 37 soldiers killed and 7 officers and 115 soldiers wounded. The last action was fought on 6 June at

Viswema, which allowed 2nd Division to move towards Imphal and complete the Allied offensive to drive back the attacking Japanese forces.

By then the monsoon had begun, and the Royals found themselves operating in conditions which tested their morale and ingenuity. In the heavy rain tracks disappeared altogether, leaving impassable quagmires; food was often in short supply; malaria was an ever-present danger; and the remaining pockets of Japanese resistance had to be cleared. It could have been a difficult phase, but with the Japanese back on the other side of the Chindwin there was the satisfaction of knowing that the enemy had been defeated. As the Japanese historian of the Burma campaign, Kojimo Noboru, put it, they were 'no longer a body of soldiers, but a herd of exhausted men', stricken by dysentery, typhus and malaria. For those on the winning side, though, it was rather different. The Royals' Padre Crichton Robertson remembered that the conditions brought out the best in the men, who refused to be down-hearted and always rallied even when 'hungry, tired, soaked to the skin with a foul night ahead of us'. And then there was a memorable moment on the return march at Kamjong, when dreams of food became reality when a mule train brought in much-needed rations after days of want. 'How we cheered! Food, and again food. Delicious bully, tasty Army biscuits; we ate everything. We had to rest at Kamjong for 24 hours to get our strength back and to digest the huge meals we had.'

The war in Burma was entering its final phase. By then the war was going badly for the Japanese in the Pacific, where US offensives had taken their forces within striking range of Japan, and the setback in Burma had left the Japanese forces isolated. For the Allies, the victory at Imphal and Kohima had demonstrated the capacity of their forces to defeat the Japanese in open battle. It had also put the enemy on the defensive. Against that background, the Allies decided on a twin assault which saw General Sir William Slim's Fourteenth Army attack the enemy on the line between Mandalay and Pakkoku (Operation Capital) while a second amphibious and airborne assault on Rangoon was planned at the beginning of 1945 (Operation Dracula). Slim's intention was to break out from the Kohima area and make a four-pronged advance towards Indaw, Schwebo, Myinmu and Pakkoku. At the same time, Lieutenant-General Sir Philip Christison's XV Corps would move back into the Arakan and capture the air fields which would extend Allied air cover to Rangoon and the border with Thailand. The offensive opened on 3 December when the 11th East African Division and the 20th Indian Division crossed the Chindwin and began advancing, with little sign of Japanese resistance. Faced with less opposition than he had expected, Slim decided to feint towards Mandalay while driving towards Meiktila, a key communications centre. Once the upper reaches of the River Irrawaddy had been seized, the way would be open to race south to Rangoon.

For the Royals, this meant taking part in 2nd Division's move towards Schwebo, which had to be cleared before moving on to Ywathitgyi on the River Irrawaddy. The latter operation provoked a hard-fought battle which the divisional commander Major-General C.G.G. Nicholson described as 'one of the most formidable Battalion tasks which my Division undertook in Burma'. Not for the first time, the Royals were taken aback by the resistance put up by the enemy in the face of a sustained attack involving aircraft and armour, but the successful outcome brought them within 30 miles of Mandalay. And, as *The Thistle* recorded, it took the battalion into a completely different landscape:

> In a zone of sun-cracked, uncultivated paddy and dry
> thorn scrub, intersected by deep powder-dust cart tracks,

we met the Burman, a cheerful, clean and colourful character with a sense of humour, but too easy-going. Patches of tall copra and toddy palms amongst vivid yellow-green banana plantations were shady and restful relief from the blistering heat and haze of the plain. Better still, these cultivated plantations usually indicated a sure source of good water and a variety of sturdily built huts. Whitewashed pagodas with gilded crests and tinkling toy bells dotted the hills and plains, amid clusters of bright flowering shrubs and guarded by enormous stones.

The road to Rangoon lay ahead. Mandalay fell to the 19th Indian Division on 13 March while the 2nd Division, attacking from the west, captured Fort Ava. During this final phase of the operations the Royals were in constant contact with the enemy, although one action almost ended in farce. After the railway station at Paleik was captured, an elaborate attack was planned on the nearby railway works at Myitnge, but no assault was needed and no shots were fired as the Japanese had already withdrawn. On 2 May the remaining Japanese were cut off in the Arakan and the next day the first units entered Rangoon following amphibious landings by the 26th Indian Division. For the Japanese in Burma the war was over and as the regiment's historian, Colonel Paterson, reminds us, the victory owed everything to the resilience of the British, Indian and Gurkha soldiers: 'It had taken several years, but in the end the Japanese Army had been beaten, fighting in its own environment.'

For The Royal Scots in Burma, it was also the end of the war. On 10 April, the 1st battalion was flown back to Chittagong and from there travelled on to Kachrapara near Calcutta where it remained until the end of the year. This allowed the demobilisation of time-served and war-enlisted men before a move to Johor Baharu on

192

the Malayan mainland close to Singapore. The regiment never returned to Burma, a country which has featured prominently in its long history, but it did not depart without leaving any trace of its presence during the Second World War. On 25 November 1944, on a site at Kennedy Hill on the Aradura Spur, the battalion unveiled a stone memorial to its dead in the fighting for Imphal and Kohima; it commemorates the names of those Royal Scots who were killed in what the Supreme Allied Commander, Admiral Lord Louis Mountbatten, called 'one of the greatest battles in history . . . it was in effect the Battle of Burma'.

TEN

BRAVE NEW WORLD:
THE COLD WAR AND AFTER

Britain ended the war with armed forces numbering just over 5,000,000 men and women in uniform, and with the same strategic obligations that it had possessed in 1939. The army alone had 20 divisions, but it very quickly became clear that the cost of maintaining those forces was beyond the reach of a country whose economy had been devastated by the war. To all intents and purposes, many things remained the same in the armed forces, but the next 20 years were to witness a sea change as their size was decreased and Britain's overseas colonial holdings were dramatically reduced. Fighting the Second World War had drained Britain financially, and Clement Attlee's post-war Labour government found itself having to grapple with the problems of recession, shortages and financial restrictions imposed by the shattered economy. In a world which saw Britain negotiating a loan of $3.75 million from the United States, followed by harsh measures to restrict domestic expenditure, huge armed forces were a luxury the country could ill afford. Between 1946 and 1948 the RAF Estimates shrank from £255.5 million to £173 million. The Naval Estimates for 1949 totalled £153 million, a decrease of £44 million on the previous year, and the government urged further economies in personnel and matériel on both services. Expenditure on the army was also reduced, from £350 million to £270 million, and Second World War equipment was not replaced in any quantity until the 1950s, forcing Field Marshal Viscount Montgomery of Alamein, Chief of the Imperial General Staff between 1946 and 1948, to remark that 'the Army was in a parlous condition, and was in a complete state of unreadiness and unpreparedness for war'.

Unlike the shambles of 1919, when it had taken undue time to release wartime conscripts and volunteers, demobilisation was carried out quickly and efficiently, so that time-served and war service personnel could return to civilian life. To replace them, conscription was kept in being. Under a succession of post-war National Service Acts, it became the law of the land for every male citizen to register at his local branch of the Ministry of Labour and National Service as soon as he became 18. Information about the relevant age-groups and clear-cut instructions were placed in the national newspapers and broadcast on BBC radio, and schools and employers also played their part in passing on the relevant official information to their young charges. Short of deliberately refusing to register, there was no way the method of call-up could be ignored and those who did try to avoid conscription were always traced through their National Health records. Between the end of the war and the phasing out of conscription in 1963, 2,300,000 men served as National Servicemen, the majority in the army. In its final form, the period of conscription was two years (there had been earlier periods of 12 and 18 months) and, like every other regiment in the British Army, The Royal Scots benefited from the contribution made by men who were the only peacetime conscripts in British history.

The other great punctuation mark of the post-war years was the decision to quit India in 1947. Nationalist feeling had been kept in check during the war, but by the end of the conflict it was clear that the country could be kept under British control only by the use of overwhelming military force. With the economy under siege and facing pressure from the United States, Attlee's government took the courageous decision to pull out of India and to divide the sub-continent into India and Pakistan. Although it was not fully recognised at the time, by granting independence to these two countries Britain had delivered a lethal blow to the whole concept of its empire. Once India had gone, there was little point in maintaining large garrisons and expensive strategic installations in the Middle East and the Mediterranean. However, Britain continued to maintain its holdings in those regions, often in the face of local opposition, with the result that the armed forces were soon involved in fighting counter-insurgency wars against terrorists or 'freedom-fighters' in countries where they had long out-stayed their welcome. As the historian Correlli Barnett described the situation in the region: 'In Palestine, Egypt, Cyprus, a dreary pattern repeated itself: murder, arson, ambush, cities divided by barbed-wire, road-blocks, searches.'

The decision to quit India was a declaration. It was the largest single possession ruled by the British and was almost an empire in its own right, so exotic and various were the land and its peoples. The lives led by the British imperialists – the civil servants, the soldiers, the businessmen, the adventurers – had become part of the British outlook, too, exerting a pull on British sentiments in ways that no other colony had ever done. After it became independent, and India and Pakistan came into being on 15 August 1947, the end of empire was certain. It was fitting, therefore, that The Royal Scots should have been part of the process for, like most of the British Army, a large part of the regiment's history had been bound up with India. In 1945, the 1ˢᵗ battalion had ended its war in Burma and proceeded to Singapore before moving in January 1947 to Karachi, where it took part in the celebrations by providing the Guard of Honour and street liners for the ceremonial marking of the official transfer of power on 14 August. The occasion could have been marred by a threat to the life of the new leader of Pakistan, Dr Muhammad Ali Jinnah, but both he and the last British Viceroy Lord Louis Mountbatten agreed that the formal procession and the official opening of the Pakistan Constituent Assembly should go ahead as planned. Mountbatten's words for the occasion were prescient: 'We who are making history today are caught and carried on in the swift current of events; there is no time to look back – there is time only to look forward.'

Four months later the Royals were on the move again. In mid-December the 1ˢᵗ battalion left Karachi, boarding the troopship SS *Empire Halladale* after marching through the city with colours flying, bayonets drawn and the pipes and drums playing. For everyone concerned it was an emotional experience. Following two centuries of service, The Royal Scots were leaving the sub-continent for the last time. On arrival in Scotland they moved into Dreghorn Camp in Edinburgh to take over the running of the Lowland Brigade Training Centre (later Number 1 Primary Training Centre), responsible for putting National Servicemen bound for the Lowland regiments through their first ten weeks of basic training. By then further changes were on the way for the army's infantry regiments. As a result of the War Office's decision to reduce the size of the infantry to 64 single-battalion regiments, the Royals' two battalions were amalgamated on 9 February 1949 at Dreghorn. After the war, the 2ⁿᵈ battalion had served in Malta and Trieste, and following 263 years' unbroken service it lost its identity in a move which was much regretted, not just by the regiment but throughout the regimental area. Under the same changes, the administration of the infantry was reorganised, with the creation of three 'category' brigades (Guards, Light Infantry and Green Jacket) and 11 'regional' brigades. For Scotland, this involved The Lowland Brigade (Royal Scots, Royal Scots Fusiliers, King's Own Scottish Borderers and Cameronians) and The Highland Brigade (Seaforth Highlanders, Queen's Own Cameron Highlanders, Black Watch, Highland Light Infantry, Gordon Highlanders, Argyll and Sutherland Highlanders).

During the period it spent training National Servicemen in Edinburgh, The Royal Scots were known as The Lowland Brigade Training Battalion and every two weeks they would receive intakes of 60 young men for a period of training which one conscript remembered as 'all rush and bull'. For the regiment, too, it was a strenuous time, for in addition to fulfilling its training role, it had to provide men for ceremonial duties, including The Royal Guard at Ballater later in the summer. All that came to an end early in 1951, when the new 1st battalion was deployed to serve with the British Army of the Rhine (BAOR) in Münster in West Germany. With the creation of the North Atlantic Treaty Organisation (NATO) in September 1949, BAOR was allotted to this new defensive alliance and the Northern Army Group in Germany (plus Norway and Denmark) came under the command of British generals. This was Britain's contribution to the post-war defence of western Europe, and in some respects Germany was to take over India's role in the affections of suceeding generations of British servicemen. In the first years, the rationale for their presence in Germany, by then divided into West and East, was not always apparent to soldiers, but following the blockade of Berlin in 1948, the confrontation between NATO and the Soviet Union became increasingly bitter and belligerent. In time, the period would be known as the Cold War, and for the rest of the century West Germany was to be a second home for the regiment.

In the summer of 1953, the 1st battalion embarked for service in Korea as part of the United Nations forces that had been deployed there three years earlier, following North Korea's invasion of its southern neighbour. At the end of 1950, China had entered the conflict, which became increasingly acrimonious, and by the time the Royals arrived in Pusan in July 1953 the fighting had reached stalemate along the 38th parallel. The majority of the UN forces were American, and the British contribution formed part of a Commonwealth Division. On arrival in the country the 1st battalion went into reserve positions near the Imjin River, scene of some of the fiercest fighting earlier in the war, and began a period of intensive training including live firing with 60mm mortars and American Browning machine-guns. With the nearest enemy positions under two miles away, the other main activities included the construction of defences, but to the consternation of the battalion no sooner had it arrived than a truce came into effect on 27 July, and the war was effectively over. Ahead lay a year's further service in the country, undertaking internal security duties and other necessary administrative tasks. It could have been a boring ordeal but as the commanding officer, Lieutenant-Colonel Mike Melvill, remembered later in an article in *The Thistle*, there was 'the curious satisfaction of having to do everything for oneself, the amount of work and time involved, and the amazing versatility shown by the modern young soldier when put to the test'.

The deployment ended in July 1954, when the battalion made its way by sea to the Suez Canal Zone, with stops at Hong Kong, Singapore, Colombo and Aden. First impressions were not good: the fly-blown, sand-strewn military bases in the Zone were forlorn and disagreeable, the climate was vile and the local population was usually hostile. Of all the postings on offer to the post-war serviceman, this was the most unpopular and it left an indelible mark on all who served there. The Zone had been created during the Second World War, and in March 1947 it had become a secure base for the British Army following Egyptian nationalist protests at the British military presence. (British forces remained in Egypt as 'guests' following a treaty signed in 1936.) By the time the Royals arrived, the British garrisons were locked in the Zone, ostensibly guarding the Suez Canal but in effect protecting themselves from outraged Egyptian nationalists, including the Bulak Nizam, paramilitary auxiliaries who had mastered the hit-and-run tactics of guerrilla warfare. By 1952 the atmosphere had worsened when the pro-British Egyptian leader King Farouk was deposed and replaced with a military council headed by Major-General Mohammed Neguib. Two years later there was further change, when Colonel Gamal Abdul Nasser, a perfervid Egyptian nationalist, seized power and served notice on Britain to quit the Zone within 20 months. During their time in the Zone, the 1st battalion's duties centred on providing guards for installations and training exercises in the desert area. The tour of duty should have ended with a return to Britain after two years overseas, but in September 1955 the 1st battalion was hurriedly and unexpectedly ordered to deploy in Cyprus.

The island had been in British possession under Ottoman sovereignty since 1878, as part of the divisions of land engineered by the Congress of Berlin, which blocked Russian territorial ambitions in the Balkans. For Benjamin Disraeli, the British Prime Minister who brokered the deal, Cyprus was envisaged as a second Malta, a strategic base in the Mediterranean which would help to protect the Suez Canal and provide a stepping-stone to the Middle East. At the outbreak of the First World War, Britain annexed the island and offered it to Greece as an inducement for helping Serbia in the fighting in the Balkans, but this was rejected and in 1925 Cyprus became a British Crown Colony governed by a legislative council. Within four years, though, there was trouble involving the local population, and three main groups had emerged, all with differing political ambitions. The Turkish minority favoured British rule until such time as the new Turkish republic could look after its interests. The Orthodox Church represented the leadership of the majority Cypriot Greeks, and favoured autonomy, while a minority group demanded union or *enosis* with Greece and by the 1930s was prepared to use violence to achieve its aims.

In the post-war period Cyprus quickly became a new battleground as Greek Cypriot guerrillas formed themselves into an underground army *Ethniki Organosis Kypriakou Agonos* (EOKA, or the National Organisation of Greek Fighters) under the command of Colonel Georgios Grivas. Not to be outdone, the Orthodox Church, led by Archbishop Makarios, gave substantial moral and political impetus to EOKA and the unrest spilled over into violence and civil disobedience. Between 1955 and 1959 the EOKA 'emergency' claimed the lives of 105 British service personnel, 50 policemen and 240 civilians. At the height of the troubles, service personnel were not allowed out of their camps unless they had an armed escort, and all the quarters on the military bases were always heavily guarded, although it has to be said that large numbers of the local population remained on relatively good terms with the British throughout the confrontation.

The 1st battalion arrived in Cyprus in September 1955 and was deployed immediately in the Paphos district in the west of the island. It quickly settled into a routine which consisted of searches for hidden weapons and operations in support of the police force. The Royal Scots' arrival coincided with the appointment of Field Marshal Sir John Harding as governor, and he began employing the same counter-insurgency methods which had proved so successful in Malaya during the long-drawn-out campaign against Communist terrorists. Operations against EOKA were intensified, with offensive sweeps and drives, and a state of emergency was declared in November. On one occasion, the 1ˢᵗ battalion came within an ace of capturing Grivas during operations in the Troodos mountains undertaken in conjunction with 45 Commando Royal Marines. Throughout the campaign, the main danger came from EOKA terrorists using grenades and bombs, and the battalion lost two soldiers in two separate attacks. In some respects, the military situation in Cyprus was to be an uneasy forerunner of later operations in Northern Ireland.

In January 1956 the Royals' tour of duty came to an end, and they handed over to 40 Commando Royal Marines before leaving by troopship for a welcome return to Scotland. For the next ten months their base was at Elgin, but although they did not know it at the time, they would be back in the Mediterranean theatre of operations before the year had ended. After coming to power in Egypt Nasser had adopted an increasingly shrill anti-Western stance, calling on his fellow Arabs to show solidarity and not to tolerate the British military presence in Jordan, Libya and Aden. (The last British regiment, 2ⁿᵈ Grenadier Guards, left the Suez Canal Zone in March 1956.) At the same time, his attitude towards Israel became more bellicose and, to Western indignation, he entered into an agreement with Czechoslovakia for the supply of Soviet military equipment. Matters came to a head on 26 July when Nasser nationalised the Suez Canal, a move which not only hit British prestige but forced all ships using the canal to pay fees to the Egyptian government and not to the British–French consortium that owned the canal.

The day after the proclamation Britain's Prime Minister, Anthony Eden, asked the Chiefs of Staff to prepare plans for an invasion and recapture of the canal in conjunction with French forces. Amongst the many problems encountered were uncertainty about the legality of going to war with Egypt, the over-stretch of the armed forces and the difficulty of creating a workable plan for an operation on which there was no common agreement. For the historians of the Chiefs of Staff, this proved to be an unhappy and frustrating time in British military history: 'They themselves [the Chiefs of Staff] were as emotionally and temperamentally divided on the Suez issues as were the Cabinet, the British electorate, and the old and new dominions of the Commonwealth.' As the summer progressed, many of the drawbacks of Britain's defence policy were exposed. Amongst the most serious were an acute shortage of landing craft, reliance on ships being taken out of reserve and the absence of the strategic reserve (16th Parachute Brigade and 3 Commando Brigade) on peacekeeping duties in Cyprus. From the outset the plans were fraught with problems and complications which quickly turned into disaster. Offensive operations did not begin until the first week of November following a successful Israeli attack on Sinai. With British complicity, France had brought Israel into the plan and encouraged them to attack across the Sinai Desert towards the canal. This allowed France and Britain to intervene as peacemakers by issuing an ultimatum to both countries to stop fighting and remove their forces from the vicinity of the canal or face the consequences of military intervention. As had been anticipated, it was an undertaking which Nasser could not accept and the first British bombers started attacking Egyptian airfields in the late afternoon of 31 October 1956. Following five days of sustained bombing attacks to destroy the Egyptian air force British and French airborne forces landed on 5 November, seized their objectives at Gamil and Port Fuad without much difficulty and paved the way for a seaborne landing at Port Said.

This is where The Royal Scots come into the story. In August its reservists had been recalled, along with 25,000 of their number, and the 1st battalion had been placed on 7 days' notice to move. They would form part of the British force which would be needed to complete the Suez operations, and it was hoped that they would be able to land unopposed. The plan bore many similarities to the Normandy operations – following the airborne assault, land forces including armoured formations would land at Port Said after a short but effective naval bombardment – and it was hoped that a short and successful attack would pave the way for decisive diplomatic action to resolve the crisis. All Egyptian resistance had been quashed by 6 November but by then the 'war' was over before it had begun. Soviet belligerence and US financial pressure forced Eden to call a ceasefire and to turn the problem over to the United Nations. It was a humiliating order which Britain had no option but to accept, as Washington had refused to support Britain's application to the International Monetary Fund for a loan to support the falling pound unless those conditions were met.

While these events were taking place the Royals were still at sea on board the troopship HMT *Empire Fowey*, and there was a good deal of uncertainty about what would happen next. In the event, the 1st battalion disembarked at Port Said on 13 November and took over the positions being held by 45 Commando, which had been one of the original invasion formations. Despite the ceasefire, the battalion found itself virtually in a war zone. Port Said was the entrance to the Suez Canal and anti-British feelings were running high in the local population, especially in the area known as Arab Town. Weapons were freely available and the danger of attacks on patrols was as high as it had been in Cyprus. At the same time, British troops had to undertake humanitarian aid operations and work in conjunction with UN forces after their deployment in mid-December. Predictably, it was a frustrating time for the regiment. It had left Britain prepared to fight in an offensive action but ended up taking part in ill-defined peacekeeping operations, knowing that its involvement had been roundly condemned by the rest of the world. The ill-advised adventure was over by 23 December, when the last British troops left Port Said on board the troopship HMT *Dunera*. Amongst them were 1st Royal Scots, who returned to their base in Elgin early in 1957. On leaving Port Said, one officer spoke for many when he noted in *The Thistle* that although they were glad to be heading for home 'many had the feeling of a naughty schoolboy being expelled from school for something he had not done'.

British casualties in Suez were 22 dead and 97 wounded, but the greatest damage had been done to the country's international standing. Egypt's neighbours in the Middle East had been outraged by the action, which had also been condemned by the UN Security Council. To make matters worse for Eden's government, the reasons for the ceasefire were widely known and the subsequent withdrawal was seen as a stunning humiliation which marked the beginning of the end of Britain's position as a global power. In the aftermath there was a rapid rethinking of British defence policy, caused not just by Suez but also by Britain's changing place in the world. This centred on the dangers of taking unilateral action, the relevance of maintaining large and ponderous conscript forces and the impact of nuclear weapons. The resulting Defence White Paper in April 1957 put forward a new policy which would enhance Britain's nuclear deterrent, end National Service, create a new strategic reserve and replace the conventional equipment so cruelly exposed at Suez. To make military service more attractive, the Griggs Advisory Committee reported the following year and recommended that service pay should be reviewed every two years, that housing should be improved and that officers should be drawn from a wider social class. However, despite those enhancements, recruiting to the army was slow and by 1962 the minimum requirement for 165,000 men had not been met, resulting in the retention of 9,000 National Servicemen to make good the deficit.

For the most part the ending of National Service was welcomed, as by then it had become unpopular with most politicians and the general public alike. However, the decision had a knock-on effect in the Territorial Army. After 1957 National Servicemen were relieved of their obligation to train with the Territorial Army, which underwent changes in its organisation in 1956, 1961 and 1967, with the formation in the latter year of the Territorial Army and Army Volunteer Reserve. As a result, the Royal Scots' two Territorial battalions were amalgamated on 1 March 1961 to form the 8/9th battalion, with its headquarters in East Claremont Street, Edinburgh, and with outlying stations in Bathgate, Broxburn, Dalkeith, Haddington, Peebles and Tranent. The changes signalled a gradual diminution in the size of the Territorial Army, and in Edinburgh the amalgamation was particularly regretted as it entailed the loss of the 7/9th's kilts, the last link with the traditions of the 'Dandy Ninth'.

The end of National Service was supposed to herald a return to a professional volunteer army, but it also meant that the army would have to work hard to find the next generations of recruits. The last conscripts had left the 1st battalion in 1962, and now the regiment had to be self-sufficient in attracting recruits, which soon turned out to be a perennial problem. As Colonel Paterson points out in in his regimental history, in the first nine months of 1963 the Royals only managed to attract 42 recruits to its ranks. As predicated by the 1957 defence review, the cost of maintaining the armed forces was gradually reduced in real terms and the size of the army fell, with the result that ten years after the end of National Service its establishment stood at 166,000, with 55,000 stationed in Germany with BAOR, organised in four (later three) armoured and one artillery divisions. Its strength had declined in real terms, but the aim was to build up skills and capabilities so that its units would be flexible enough to operate anywhere in the world. For senior soldiers of that period such as Major-General John Strawson, the watchword was that 'although small, the army led the world in experience'. That was certainly the experience of The Royal Scots. Following an enjoyable posting to Libya (from October 1960 to April 1963), the 1st battalion was posted to Tidworth, where it became part of the 51st Infantry Brigade Group in the 3rd Division, and part of the newly created United Kingdom Strategic Reserve. In that role it trained for rapid deployment to trouble-spots overseas, and that entailed learning new skills working in conjunction with the RAF.

In 1964, the 1st battalion demonstrated its new versatility when it was ordered to deploy to Aden to take part in the operations against insurgent tribesmen in the Radfan, the mountainous border region adjacent to Yemen. The trouble had started with the creation of the British-sponsored Federation of South Arabia, a combination of the colony of Aden and the 20 various sheikhdoms and emirates in the area, to prepare them for independence. In January 1964, three battalions of the Aden Federal Army (FRA) had attempted to put down a tribal revolt in the Radfan which had been aided and abetted by the Arab National Liberation Front (NLF), itself sponsored by Egypt, but it had become quickly bogged down, hence the need for reinforcements. For the first time, the Royals were flown to the trouble-spot, travelling from RAF Lyneham in Britannia aircraft which took 22 hours to reach Aden, including refuelling stops at Akrotiri in Cyprus and at Bahrain. Following acclimatisation, the battalion was in its operational area during the second week in June, by which time the main operation to subdue the Radfan had been completed, with the capture of its highest point, Jebel Huriyah. That success did not mean that hostilities were over. Far from it: for the next three years dissident activity continued unabated and the battalion was in the thick of the action.

The campaign in the Radfan was a real test for the Royals. Not only was the topography harsh and the weather conditions unpredictable, but The Royal Scots faced a hidden enemy who used a wide variety of tactics. To counter them, the battalion patrolled constantly and laid ambushes to prevent movement; skills developed at Tidworth came into their own, not least the use of forward air controllers to call down strikes by RAF Hunter strike aircraft. Thanks to the use of military helicopters, the battalion was able to overcome many of the difficulties imposed by the terrain. During the deployment there were also four tours of duty in Aden town, which had become the main focus for NLF attacks. By then, the terrorists had become more sophisticated and were using booby traps and mines to attack British installations but, despite a number of incidents, the Royals sustained no casualties. The battalion's one loss was a soldier killed in a motoring accident. It had been a long and gruelling tour, but the battalion returned to Tidworth in January 1965 fitter and more experienced than it had been before the deployment. A year later it moved to Osnabruck in Germany to face a fresh challenge as a mechanised battalion equipped with the new FV-432 Tracked Fighting Vehicle, capable of carrying a platoon into battle.

The conversion programme was a challenge but the battalion rose to it and quickly settled down to the BAOR operational year. At the end of 1969 there was a further change when it was deployed for the first emergency tour of Northern Ireland in support of the Royal Ulster Constabulary. This was in answer to the request made by the government of Northern Ireland in August 1969 for the provision of troops to assist the civil power in restoring order following outbreaks of sectarian violence in Belfast and

Londonderry. All told, between then and 1999 the battalion was to experience 11 operational tours in Northern Ireland, together with two residential tours of two years' duration at Ballykinler and Ballykelly. Each tour brought its own challenges in helping to keep the peace and maintain a sense of proportion in one of the most difficult and long-lasting counter-insurgency wars fought by the British Army. The main opponents were the Provisional Irish Republican Army (PIRA) but trouble was also fomented by unionist terrorist groups and other troublemakers. The war lasted until the 1990s and during that period The Royal Scots continued to have other commitments. In 1974, after four further years at Tidworth as part of the Allied Command Europe's mobile forces, the battalion was back in Cyprus to protect the Western Sovereign Base Area created after the island had become independent in 1959. In March 1983 the regiment celebrated its 350th anniversary, and it was announced that HRH Princess Anne would be the regiment's new Colonel-in-Chief in succession to her predecessor HRH The Princess Royal, a daughter of King George V, who had been Colonel-in-Chief from 1918 until her death in 1965. There were also further tours with BAOR – Münster between 1976 and 1979 in the nuclear escort role, and Werl between 1985 and 1991 in the mechanised role. In 1989 the 1st battalion started re-equipping with the new Warrior Infantry Fighting Vehicle, a period which *The Thistle* described as producing a breakthrough in the regiment's capabilities: 'For the first time in our history we have been equipped with an infantry-fighting vehicle that has such outstanding mobility, protection and firepower that we are having to rethink the whole philosophy of warfare.'

Within a year, The Royal Scots would need to summon all their experience and resilience when the 1st battalion was deployed to Saudi Arabia in December 1991. The move was made as part of

Operation Granby, the British contribution to the US-led United Nations forces which had been dispatched to Saudi Arabia following the invasion and occupation of Kuwait by Iraqi forces on 2 August 1990. It was followed by a lengthy game of diplomatic cat-and-mouse carried out by the UN Security Council and Iraq's leader President Saddam Hussein which culminated with the issue of Resolution 678. This gave the Iraqis until 15 January 1991 to pull out of Kuwait. At the same time, armed forces were deployed in Saudi Arabia and the Gulf region in preparation for offensive operations to oust Iraqi forces. The battalion arrived in Saudi over the Christmas and New Year period, and from the outset the commanding officer, Lieutenant-Colonel Iain Johnstone, ensured that it was put on, and then retained, the discipline of a full war footing. Under his command, The Royal Scots battle group also had a company from The Grenadier Guards and Milan detachments from 1st Queen's Own Highlanders, and shortly before the land war began he was able to report that the battalion had 'built up a reputation of such strength that even the other units are frightened of us'.

In the land operations which began on 24 February, the 1st Royal Scots fought in 4th Armoured Brigade, 1st British Armoured Division under the overall command of Major-General Rupert Smith. Before they went into the attack, their orders were changed to take on and destroy an Iraqi artillery regiment at a position codenamed BRONZE before moving on to engage a more heavily defended brigade-sized position codenamed BRASS. Before the assault, the Iraqi positions were hit by air strikes and artillery fire, but there was almost a mishap as the battalion crossed the start line only to see their way blocked by slow-moving ammunition trucks belonging to 26 Field Regiment Royal Artillery. Even so, the battalion's attack on BRONZE was a complete success. The first contact was made by the Challenger tanks of the accompanying squadron of Life Guards, while the battalion began the messy job of clearing and securing the bunkers. It took four hours to take the position, and during the fighting the battalion took large numbers of Iraqi prisoners, a factor which slowed down the pace of its advance.

The next objective was BRASS which contained a brigade-sized force but 4th Brigade had surprise on its side. Following a heavy artillery barrage, the attack went in from the north, with The Royal Scots attacking the western sector and the 3rd Royal Regiment of Fusiliers attacking the eastern sector, while the tanks of 14/20 Hussars engaged the centre with the support of the Grenadiers' Warriors as the infantry element. The Royals took their objective quickly and efficiently with a four-pronged attack on 26 February, in which they destroyed large numbers of Iraqi armoured vehicles and tanks and took 80 prisoners. For his exceptional bravery during the action, clearing Iraqi bunkers with grenades, Private Thomas Gow of B Company was awarded the Military Medal. Also honoured were Majors Norman Soutar and John Potter, who received the Military Cross. The battalion's next objective was codenamed TUNGSTEN, some 30 kilometres away. It was attacked and cleared the next day following light Iraqi resistance, and the end of the 100-hour war was in sight. A ceasefire was declared at 8.00 a.m. on 28 February, and two days later the UN adopted Resolution 686, which called for the 'suspension of offensive combat operations'. At the end of the month the battalion began moving back to Werl, having taken part in what Johnstone called 'an amazing experience'.

On the Royals' arrival in Germany there was a period of well-deserved leave before starting preparations to move back to Fort George in Scotland but the 'feel-good factor' did not last long. Four months later came the astonishing news that The Royal Scots was to be amalgamated with The King's Own Scottish Borderers. It was no secret that there were going to be cutbacks and amalgamations in the army. The previous summer, the government had produced its Defence White Paper, *Options for Change*, which proposed that the army should be reduced from 155,000 to 116,000 soldiers and that the infantry should lose 17 of its 55 battalions. The cuts came as a result of the end of the Cold War, following the disintegration of the Soviet Union and the reunification of the two Germanys. It was accepted that Scottish regiments would be affected, but following the Royals' service in the Gulf the decision came as a shattering blow and immediate steps were taken by the regiment to fight it. A well-organised and high-profile campaign was initiated and as a result the amalgamation was cancelled on 3 February 1993, together with the proposed amalgamation of the Cheshire and Staffordshire Regiments. At the time, the battalion was serving in South Armagh and on its return it was immediately obvious that the decline in recruiting – one of the reasons for the amalgamation – would have to be addressed and corrected.

Alas, the reprieve was to be short-lived. Twelve years later, under the terms of the new Strategic Defence Review of July 2004, it was announced that as a result of a decision to reduce the size of the infantry still further, The Royal Scots would, after all, amalgamate with The King's Own Scottish Borderers. Unsurprisingly, given the attachment that Scots feel for their regiments, the decision was not welcomed by everyone and, once again, determined efforts were made to save Scotland's regiments. The moment was also made more poignant by the fact that the 1st battalion was deployed to serve in Iraq in January 2006 as part of Britain's military commitment to the forces in the country following the operations to depose Saddam Hussein in 2003. Once again, it seemed that a historic and highly regarded regiment was bearing the brunt of unnecessary defence cuts and

APPENDIX

REGIMENTAL FAMILY TREE

1633–1637: Le Regiment de Hebron (in French service)

1637–1678: Le Regiment de Douglas (in French service)

1678–1684: Earl of Dumbarton's Regiment of Foot (in British service)

1684–1751: The Royal Regiment of Foot (also known as Douglas's, Orkney's and St Clair's); 2nd battalion raised 1686

1751–1812: 1st or Royal Regiment of Foot; 3rd and 4th battalions raised 1804

1812–1821: 1st Regiment of Foot or Royal Scots

1822–1871: 1st or The Royal Regiment of Foot; 3rd and 4th battalions disbanded 1817

1871–1881: 1st or The Royal Scots Regiment

1881–1882: The Lothian Regiment (Royal Scots)

1882–1920: The Royal Scots (Lothian Regiment)

1920–2006: The Royal Scots (The Royal Regiment); 1st and 2nd battalions amalgamated 1949

2006: The Royal Scots Borderers, 1st Battalion The Royal

Regiment of Scotland; amalgamation with The King's Own Scottish Borderers

REGIMENTAL BADGE

With several variations, the badge of The Royal Scots is the Star of the Order of the Thistle, in the centre St Andrew and his cross, worn on a red cloth background. The motto is *Nemo me impune lacessit* (No one provokes me with impunity).

REGIMENTAL TARTANS

In the early years of its service with the British Army, The Royal Scots wore the standard red coat (with blue facings) and white kersey breeches worn by all soldiers. It was not until the reforms of 1881 when they were renamed The Lothian Regiment (Royal Scots) that they were issued with the tartan trews of the Government or 'Black Watch' Tartan to signify that they were a Scottish regiment. It was introduced on 1 April 1882. In 1901 approval was given for the tartan to be changed to the Hunting Stuart tartan although this was not worn until the regiment returned from the Boer War.

At the time of the regiment's tercentenary in 1933, King George V conferred on the regiment's pipers the right to wear his personal tartan, the Royal Stuart tartan. The only battalion to wear the kilt was the 9th (Highland) battalion, which was raised during the Boer War and served with great distinction throughout the First World War. Known as the 'Dandy Ninth', it was a Territorial Force battalion and it recruited mainly from men with Highland backgrounds living in the city of Edinburgh.

REGIMENTAL PIPE MUSIC

From its beginnings, The Royal Scots have used pipers as well as the fifes and drums which were employed throughout the army in the seventeenth and eighteenth centuries. The pipes and drums were always fully trained infantry soldiers and were in addition to the military band, which existed until 1994, when it was disbanded to form the Band of the Lowland Division. The regiment's pipe music was regularised as follows:

> March in quick time: Dumbarton's Drums, Daughter of
>   the Regiment (played when royalty are on parade)
> March in slow time: The Garb of Old Gaul
> March on and Fall in: Scotland the Brave
> Advance in Review Order: Scotland the Brave
> March on with Military Band: Scots Royal
> Royal Salute: Point of War
> General Salute: Loch Leven Castle
> The Charge: Monymusk
> March off: Blue Bonnets over the Border

COMPANY MARCHES

A Company: The Barren Rocks of Aden
B Company: Mhairi's Wedding
C Company: The Black Bear
Headquarter Company: The Steamboat

BATTLE HONOURS

Since 1743, The Royal Scots have carried two colours, the King's or Queen's, which was the Union flag and the Regimental (originally First and Second Colour), which was dark blue in colour, with the Union flag in the upper centre and the regimental cypher in the centre. Four years later, in 1747, the warrant was amended to read: 'First Regiment, or the Royal Regiment. In the centre of their colours, the King's cypher within the circle of St Andrew and Crown over it; in the three corners of the 2nd Colour, the Thistle and Crown.'

During the Napoleonic Wars, battle honours were added to the colours. In their final form, those gained during the First World War and the Second World War are carried on the Queen's Colour and the remainder are carried on the Regimental Colour (the Union flag was removed in the late nineteenth century). At the outset, battle honours were given sparingly or even randomly: The Royal Scots' first honour was given in 1801 and consisted of the Sphinx and the word 'Egypt' to mark the 2nd battalion's role in the campaign against Napoleon.

In 1882, the system of battle honours was revised by a War Office committee under the chairmanship of General Sir Archibald Alison. It laid down guidelines whereby only victories would be included and the majority of the regiment had to be present. Additional refinements were made in 1907 and 1909, and their recommendations form the basis of the regiment's pre-1914 battle honours.

1633–1913
1st, 2nd and 3rd battalions

Tangier 1680	Corunna	Maheidpor
Namur 1695	Busaco	Ava
Blenheim	Salamanca	Alma
Ramillies	Vittoria	Inkerman
Oudenarde	St Sebastian	Sevastopol
Malplaquet	Nive	Taku Forts
Louisburg	Peninsula	Peking 1860
Havana	Niagara	South Africa 1899–1902
Egmont-op-Zee	Waterloo	
St Lucia 1803	Nagpore	

THE FIRST WORLD WAR

35 battalions

Mons

Le Cateau

Retreat from Mons

Marne, 1914, 1918

Aisne 1914

La Bassee 1914

Neuve Chapelle

Ypres 1915, 1917, 1918

Gravenstafel

St Julien

Frezenburg

Bellewaarde

Aubers

Festubert 1915

Loos

Somme 1916, 1918

Albert 1916, 1918

Bazentin

Pozieres

Flers-Courcelette

Le Transloy

Ancre Heights

Ancre 1916, 1918

Arras 1917, 1918

Arleux

Pilckem

Langemarck 1917

Menin Road

Polygon Wood

Poelcappelle

Passchendaele

Cambrai 1917

Scarpe 1917, 1918

St Quentin

Rosieres

Lys

Estaires

Messines 1918

Hazebrouck

Bailleul

Kemmel

Bethune

Soissonnais-Ourcq

Tardenois

Amiens

Bapaume 1918

Drocourt-Queant

Hindenburg Line

St Quentin Canal

Beaurevoir

Courtrai

Selle

Sambre

France and Flanders 1914–18

Struma

Canal du Nord

Macedonia 1915–18

Helles

Landing at Helles

Krithia

Suvla

Scimitar Hill

Gallipoli 1915, 1916

Rumani

Egypt 1915–16

Gaza

El Mughar

Nebi Samwil

Jaffa

Palestine 1917–18

Archangel 1918–19

After the First World War there were further refinements to take cognisance of the size and complexity of the conflict. It was agreed that each regiment could carry ten major honours on their King's Colour, but supporting operations would also receive battle honours which would not be displayed on the colours. The battle honours in bold type are carried on the Queen's Colour.

THE SECOND WORLD WAR
1st, 2nd, 7/9th, 8th battalions

Dyle	Meijil	Marradi
Defence of Escaut	Venlo Pocket	Monte Gamberaldi
St Omer–La Bassee	Roer	**Italy 1944–45**
Odon	Rhineland	South East Asia 1941
Cheux	Reichswald	Donbaik
Defence of Rauray	Cleve	**Kohima**
Caen	Goch	Relief of Kohima
Esquay	**Rhine**	Aradura
Mont Pincon	Uelzen	Schwebo
Aart	Bremen	Mandalay
Nederrijn	Artlenberg	**Burma 1943–45**
Best	**North-West Europe**	
Scheldt	**1940, 1944–45**	
Flushing	**Gothic Line**	

In 1956 it was agreed to treat the Second World War in the same way as the earlier conflict. Those in bold type appear on the Queen's Colour.

POST-1945
1st battalion
Gulf 1991
Wadi Al Batin

The battle honours gained since 1945, in bold type, are carried on the Regimental Colour.

AFFILIATED REGIMENT
Royal Gurkha Rifles

ALLIED REGIMENTS
Canadian Army
The Canadian Scottish Regiment (Princess Mary's)
The Royal Newfoundland Regiment

WINNERS OF THE VICTORIA CROSS
Private Joseph Prosser, 2ⁿᵈ Royal Scots, Crimean War, 1855
His courage in two incidents outside Sevastopol led to the award
of the Victoria Cross, which was instituted by Royal Warrant in
1856 to recognise 'most conspicuous bravery, or some daring or
pre-eminent act of valour or self-sacrifice or extreme devotion to
duty'. The first came on 18 June 1855, when Prosser chased and
apprehended a would-be deserter under fire from the Russian
lines. In the second incident, on 11 August, he exposed himself
to enemy fire to bring in a wounded soldier of the 95ᵗʰ Regiment
who was lying in an exposed position. Prosser was born in Ireland
in 1828 and died in Liverpool in 1867.

*Private Henry Howey Robson, 2ⁿᵈ Royal Scots, First World
War, 1914*
By the end of the first year of the First World War, stalemate had
come to the Western Front as the Allies and the Germans faced
one another across the fields of Flanders in hurriedly constructed
trench systems. On 14 December 1914 Private Robson, a regular
soldier, rescued a wounded non-commissioned officer during
a German attack on the British lines near Kemmel. A second
rescue attempt had to be abandoned after he was wounded whilst
'exposed to severe fire'. Robson survived his wounds and returned
to the battalion, only to be wounded again during the final stages

of the Battle of the Somme in November 1916.

A native of South Shields in County Durham, Robson later sold his medal for £80 to pay for his fare to emigrate to Canada in 1923. Eventually he became a Canadian citizen and died in Toronto in 1964, aged 69.

Lance Corporal William Angus, 8th Royal Scots, First World War, 1915

Although Angus started his military career as a Territorial soldier in the 8th Highland Light Infantry, he was awarded the Victoria Cross while serving with The Royal Scots during the Artois offensive. (Following the disbandment of the battalion two of its companies were transferred to 7th and 8th Royal Scots.) On 12 June 1915 he left his trench under heavy enemy fire to rescue an officer, and brought him back to safety even though he had been warned that his action meant certain death.

Born in Annandale, West Lothian, Angus survived the war (as did the wounded officer) and died in Carluke in 1971, aged 71.

Private Robert Dunsire, 13th Royal Scots, First World War, 1915

Dunsire won his Victoria Cross during the Battle of Loos, first serious offensive battle of 1915. His citation reads: 'For the most conspicuous bravery on Hill 70 on 26 September 1915, Private Dunsire went out under very heavy fire and rescued a wounded man from between the firing lines. Later, when another man considerably nearer the German lines was shouting for help, he crawled out again, with utter disregard to the enemy's fire, and carried him in also. Shortly afterwards the Germans attacked over this ground.'

A miner in peacetime, Dunsire was born at Buckhaven in Fife, but moved with his family to Kirkcaldy. Although he survived the

Battle of Loos, he was killed on 31 January 1916 during a German attack, and is buried in Mazingarbe Military Cemetery.

Captain Henry Reynolds, 12ᵗʰ Royal Scots, First World War, 1917

Already the holder of the Military Cross, Captain Reynolds was awarded the Victoria Cross for his 'most conspicuous bravery' while attacking an enemy pill-box (machine-gun post) on 20 September 1917. After failing to hit it with a grenade, he crawled up to the entrance and managed to push a phosphorous grenade inside, setting the pill-box on fire. Three Germans were killed and the rest surrendered with their weapons. In a second assault on another position he captured seventy prisoners and two more machine guns.

Reynolds joined The Royal Scots from The Northamptonshire Yeomanry, and after the war was recommended for a regular commission, serving until 1927 with the 2ⁿᵈ Loyal Regiment. For the rest of his life he lived and worked in southern England, and died at Carshalton in Surrey in 1948.

Private Hugh McIver, 2ⁿᵈ Royal Scots, First World War, 1918

A company runner with C Company, McIver had already shown complete disregard for his safety carrying messages under heavy fire during the second Battle of the Somme. East of Courcelles-le-Comte on 23 August 1918, he pursued a German scout into an enemy machine-gun post where he killed six Germans and captured twenty prisoners and two machine guns. According to the citation 'this gallant action enabled the company to advance unchecked'. Later in the fighting he was responsible for stopping a British tank from firing on British troops.

Already the holder of the Military Medal and bar for his bravery during the Battle of the Somme in 1916, McIver was killed in action on 2 September 1918 and is buried at Vraucourt Military Cemetery near Bapaume. A native of Linwood in Renfrewshire, where he worked as a miner, McIver had been one of the first volunteers in August 1914.

Corporal Roland Edward Elcock, 11th Royal Scots, First World War, 1918

A native of Wolverhampton, Elcock had volunteered in June 1915 whilst still under-age and served in the South Staffordshire Regiment until he was discharged and transferred home after War Office Instruction ACI 1186 allowed parents to reclaim their under-age sons from front-line service. That did not deter young Elcock, who re-enlisted in June 1917 and was quickly promoted corporal after winning the Military Medal. He was awarded the Victoria Cross during the Battle of the Selle whilst in charge of a Lewis gun team near Capelle-Ste-Catherine. On 15 October 1918, displaying initiative and great personal courage he attacked two enemy gun positions which were causing heavy casualties and preventing the British advance. Both guns were put out of action and later in the day near the River Lys he successfully attacked and disabled another gun position.

After the war Elcock worked in India, where he eventually became Director-General of Posts and Telegraphs in the North-West Frontier Province. He died at Dehra Dun in October 1944 while serving as an officer in the Indian army.

Lieutenant David Stuart Macgregor, 6th Royal Scots, First World War, 1918

Attached to the 29th Battalion Machine Gun Corps, Lieutenant Macgregor was awarded the Victoria Cross while in command of machine guns during an advance by the 1st Border Regiment near Hoogemolen in Belgium. Having found that the ground ahead was open and under heavy enemy fire he ordered his men to move forward by a safer route. At the same time, he mounted a limber and ordered the driver to leave cover and gallop forward to divert the attention of the German gunners. Once his machine guns were in position they were able to engage the enemy, and by subduing enemy fire the advance was resumed. An hour later, Macgregor was killed in action.

A product of George Watson's and George Heriot's schools in Edinburgh, Macgregor was a pre-war Territorial soldier in The Royal Field Artillery, and on the outbreak of hostilities he volunteered for overseas service and was commissioned in The Royal Scots in 1915. He is buried in Staceghem Communal Cemetery at Harlebeke in Belgium.

SELECT BIBLIOGRAPHY

Unless otherwise stated in the text, all extracts from soldiers' diaries or letters are in the possession of the regiment or lodged in the Imperial War Museum, London. Battalion and Brigade War Diaries are held in the National Archives, Kew.

BOOKS ABOUT THE ROYAL SCOTS

Alexander, Jack, *McCrae's Battalion: The Story of the 16th Royal Scots*, Mainstream, Edinburgh, 2003

Brander, A.M., *The Royal Scots* (Famous Regiments Series), Leo Cooper, London, 1976

Cannon, Richard, *Historical Record of the First or Royal Regiment of Foot*, Furnivall and Parker, London, 1847

Ewing, John, *The Royal Scots 1914–1919*, 2 vols, Oliver and Boyd, Edinburgh, 1925

Leask, J.C., and McCance, H.M., *The Regimental Records of The Royal Scots*, Alexander Thom, Dublin, 1915

McBain, S.W., *A Regiment at War: The Royal Scots 1939–1945*, Pentland Press, Edinburgh, 1988

227

Milner, Laurie, *Royal Scots in the Gulf,* Leo Cooper, London, 1994

Muir, Augustus, *The First of Foot: The History of The Royal Scots,* William Blackwood, Edinburgh, 1961

Paterson, Robert H., *Pontius Pilate's Bodyguard: A History of the First or The Royal Regiment of Foot, The Royal Scots (The Royal Regiment),* 2 vols, RHQ Royal Scots, Edinburgh, 2000

Simpson, H.J., *Three Hundred Years: The Royal Scots (The Royal Regiment),* Skinner, Edinburgh, 1933

Weaver, Lawrence, *The Story of The Royal Scots (The Lothian Regiment),* George Newnes, London, 1925

OTHER BOOKS CONSULTED

Allen, Louis, *The Longest War, 1941–1945,* J.M. Dent, London, 1984

Ascoli, David, *A Companion to the British Army 1660–1983,* Harrap, London, 1983

Barnett, Correlli, *Britain and Her Army 1509–1970,* Allen Lane, London, 1970

Baynes, John, with Laffin, John, *Soldiers of Scotland,* Brassey's, London, 1988

Blake, George, *Mountain and Flood: History of the 52nd (Lowland) Division 1939–1946,* Jackson and Son, Glasgow, 1950

Brereton, J.M., *The British Army: A Social History of the British Army from 1661 to the Present Day,* Bodley Head, London, 1986

Chandler, David, and Beckett, Ian, eds, *The Oxford Illustrated History of the British Army,* Oxford University Press, Oxford, 1994

Churchill, Winston, *A History of the English-Speaking Peoples,* vol. III, Cassell, London, 1957

Ewing, John, *History of the 9th (Scottish) Division 1914–1919,* John Murray, London, 1921

Fortescue, Sir John, *A History of the British Army*, 13 vols, Macmillan, London, 1899–1930

Henderson, Diane, *The Scottish Regiments*, Collins, Glasgow, 1996

Holmes, Richard, ed., *The Oxford Companion to Military History*, Oxford University Press, Oxford, 2001; *Sahib: The British Soldier in India*, HarperCollins, London, 2005

Jackson, Bill and Bramall, Dwin, *The Chiefs: The Story of the United Kingdom Chiefs of Staff*, Brassey's, London, 1992

Keegan, John, *Six Armies in Normandy*, Penguin, London, 1982

Laffin, John, *Scotland the Brave: The Story of the Scottish Soldier*, Brassey's, London, 1963

Martin, H.G., *The Fifteenth Scottish Division 1939–1945*, William Blackwood, Edinburgh, 1948

Mileham, P.J.R., *Scottish Regiments*, Spellmount, Tunbridge Wells, 1988

Royle, Trevor, *The Best Years of Their Lives: The National Service Experience 1945–1963*, Michael Joseph, London, 1986

Stewart, J, and Buchan, John, *The 15th (Scottish) Division 1914–1919*, William Blackwood, Edinburgh, 1926

Strawson, John, *Gentlemen in Khaki: The British Army 1890–1990*, Hutchinson, London, 1989; *Beggars in Red: The British Army 1789–1889*, Hutchinson, London, 1991

Thompson, R.R., *The Fifty-Second (Lowland) Division 1914–1918*, MacLehose Jackson, Glasgow, 1923

Wood, Stephen, *The Scottish Soldier*, Archive Publications, Manchester, 1987

Young, Derek, *Forgotten Scottish Voices from the Great War*, Tempus, Stroud, 2005

INDEX